21ˢᵗ Century Fraud

How to Protect Yourself in the New Millennium

21st Century Fraud

How to Protect Yourself in the New Millennium

Tony Lesce

Loompanics Unlimited
Port Townsend, Washington

Neither the author nor the publisher assumes any responsibility for the use or misuse of information contained in this book. It is sold for entertainment purposes only. Be Warned!

21st Century Fraud
  How to Protect Yourself in the New Millennium
© 2000 by Tony Lesce

Published by:
Loompanics Unlimited
PO Box 1197
Port Townsend, WA 98368
Loompanics Unlimited is a division of Loompanics Enterprises, Inc.
Phone: 360-385-2230
E-mail: service@loompanics.com
Web site: www.loompanics.com

ISBN 1-55950-210-X
Library of Congress Card Catalog Number 00-108962

Contents

Introduction

What are your chances of being murdered this year? We have about 20,000 murders a year in the United States, a country with almost 300 million people, and this means that your chances of escaping homicide are very good. What are your chances of being victimized by fraud? Much greater, so much greater that it's almost impossible to measure the risk. There is no central clearinghouse with all the data regarding identity theft, a common type of high-tech fraud.[1] Identity theft is only one type of fraud, although it ties in with other fraud schemes. There are many other scams operating, and the law enforcement establishment simply doesn't have a handle on them.

Frauds are far more common than street crimes. There are a wide variety of frauds, some old, and some new ones resulting from new technology and social changes. Internet fraud, a relatively new phenomenon, has been increasing exponentially.

Cops can't cope with frauds, because they are preoccupied with street crimes and violent crimes, and just don't have the expertise to fight high-tech frauds.

This book will inform you about basic fraud techniques, so you will know what the dangers are. It will also give you the information to protect yourself from fraud.

If you have a credit card, you're wide open to credit card fraud. If you don't, you're still vulnerable because identity thieves can order cards in your name and leave you stuck with the bills. You're vulnerable to phony charity fraud, check forgery, telemarketing scams, Internet scams, and other recently developed frauds born of technological advances. Frauds are rampant, and more pervasive, than street crimes.

The old tried-and-true frauds are still with us, but a rash of new frauds has arrived because of technological progress and social change. Years ago we did not have to worry about credit card fraud because nobody had credit cards. The Internet did not exist. Organized crime was very primitive, and there was no such thing as international organized crime cartels. Today, most people have credit cards, the result of aggressive marketing by credit card companies. Many Americans are on the Internet, some to browse and others to shop, and Internet fraud today is ahead of the ability of law enforcement agencies to cope. There exist many international criminal organizations, veritable multinational crime cartels that are larger and more powerful than some governments. Indeed, many multinational crime cartels own their host governments, selecting undeveloped countries as bases because their governments are vulnerable to corruption.

Cultural and social changes also have opened more windows of opportunity for fraud artists. One benefit of our affluent society is that today more Americans are traveling, booking tours and cruises, than ever before. This has led to a variety of travel scams perpetrated by fraud artists, made easier by the telephone and the Internet.

According to the Fraud Advisory Panel of the Institute of Chartered Accountants, an English professional society, it's hard to quantify the amount of fraud perpetrated because it's often under-reported. Much fraud is for small amounts, but very widespread. Business owners and managers are reluctant to report that they've been scammed, preferring to absorb the loss instead of prosecuting and running the risk of adverse publicity.[2]

Business owners today are vulnerable to the same old frauds they always were, as well as a vast array of new ones. Falsifying time cards, faking expense accounts, and conducting personal business, including phone calls, on company time are tried-and-true methods of scamming an employer. However, any company that uses the Internet can expect to be vulnerable to new methods of fraud directly linked to this technological marvel.

Internet fraud rose by 600 percent during 1998, according to the National Consumers League. This isn't surprising, given the explosive growth of Internet use during the last few years. The U.S. Congress' General Accounting Office reported that Social Security number misuse investigations increased more than 300 percent from 1996 to 1997. These figures provide only a glimpse into the amount of fraud in the United States, because each type of fraud is investigated and reported separately.

Why Cops Can't Cope

The police are not prepared to fight effectively against fraud for many reasons. One is the flood of street crime, which keeps the cops busy. In some high-risk urban areas, police are so saturated that some residents say: "Send for a pizza, then send for a cop. See which comes first."

In another vein, the government takes more steps to protect itself and its institutions than it does to safeguard its citizens. A criminal who counterfeits money will find more law officers arrayed against him than one who forges credit cards. Someone who threatens the President will get more law enforcement attention than someone who threatens you. Bet on it!

"Street crime" is going down for several reasons. The most important one is that the criminal justice system is keeping thugs in prison longer than before. Behind bars, they may victimize each other, but they cannot victimize citizens outside the walls, with a few exceptions. Another is that the population is growing older. There's a smaller proportion in the 16-25 age group, the one that contributes the most to street crime.

Another reason is that criminal predators are getting smarter as they're getting older. They learn that sticking up a "Stop and Rob" for fifty dollars can bring a five-year prison sentence. In prison, they learn new ways of earning dishonest bucks, and they learn that non-violent crime is more remunerative and has a much bigger payoff. Operating a white-collar scam is both healthier and more rewarding, and at times it's not even illegal! In fact, white-collar scams are the choice of many older criminals, who are smarter and more mature than youngsters, having learned their trade in the "crime colleges" we call prisons.

Police are slow to respond to emergency calls. They're even slower at responding to fraud complaints. Let's look more closely at this, and how the police are increasingly unprepared to cope with fraud and "white-collar crime."

Although FBI statistics show that crime has been dropping for roughly the last ten years, the FBI keeps statistics on only "index crimes," which are murder, arson, rape, auto theft, burglary, larceny, and assault. These are street crimes, including violent crimes. However, street crime also includes prostitution, illegal drug dealing, and other illegal acts not included in the FBI's Index Crimes. While the official crime rate keeps dropping, other crimes are increasing, as we'll see.

Let's look at the way our own government cons us, taking the example of official FBI figures. The government is out to convince the American people that it is effective in protecting the public against crime. This is why the FBI "index crimes" include mainly the types of crimes that are decreasing. Other types of crimes keep growing, but the government doesn't count them. It's a parallel with the government's cost-of-living index. The government claims that inflation is only one or two percent a year, a claim totally mystifying to those of us who go to the supermarket or stop at the gas station each week. We see prices ratcheting upward, despite official government assurances that they're almost stable. The Department of Commerce does not include the cost of food and fuel, because these prices are "volatile."

Now let's get back to what the FBI doesn't count in its official figures. FBI figures also do not include various rackets such as the Nigerian scams that have victimized many Americans. They do not include many "insider" thefts that have victimized employers and which employers rarely report because they fear that the news will shake public confidence in their companies. "Insider" thefts include theft of intellectual property such as proprietary information that an insider can carry out in his briefcase or steal from his employer's computer.

"Hacking" into computers to steal lists of credit card numbers is another kind of techno-crime that receives little public attention, although it's the concern of company security directors who find themselves assailed by this kind of electronic theft.

Another reason for downplaying non-violent crimes lies within our culture and value system. We consider crimes against the person, such as murder and rape, more important than crimes against property, for good reason. Property can often be replaced, while murder is final and rape leaves severe emotional scars. Thus, police assign much lower priority to frauds and thefts than they do to crimes against the person.

Yet another reason comes from the fragmentation of American law enforcement, divided into many small jurisdictions and with little cooperation between law enforcement agencies.

Criminals easily work across state lines and the cops lose valuable time deciding who has jurisdiction over their crimes. A telephone scam, for example, operates from a "boiler room" in one state, using wide-area lines to perpetrate their frauds on people in different states. By the time police find them, they've moved to another location.

Many police organizations do not have the expertise to combat credit card and other high-tech frauds. To be successful, a police effort against this type of crime has to be both well-organized and timely.[3]

Law enforcement is almost always behind the power curve when fighting scammers. Fraud artists stay at least one step ahead of the law because they are agile and fast-moving. An example was the "cloning" of cellular phone numbers to obtain free airtime. When the cellular phone companies adopted electronic countermeasures to make this more difficult, the scammers switched to identity theft to obtain accounts in the names of real people.[4] We'll see this theme again and again in these pages.

One thing that hasn't changed is that con artists are still trying to deny that they're guilty of anything. Clinging to slogans such as "You can't cheat an honest man," they claim that their victims make themselves vulnerable precisely because they are venal and avaricious. In reality, as we'll see, fraud artists devise various techniques to victimize those who are not venal, and even altruists. With a plethora of phony charities and front organizations, con men assure themselves of a good living at the expense of mainstream people.

Not all the news is bad. Some scams are rarely used today, because scientific advances have made it extremely difficult to promote them. The old trick of a pregnant woman persuading a man to marry her by falsely claiming that he's the father of her child is almost unknown today, because modern DNA testing can prove conclusively whether or not a person is the parent of a child.

What This Book Will Do for You

This book will provide you with information about the basics of fraud techniques, to give you an awareness of what the dangers are. It will also explain the techniques fraud artists use to steal your assets, enabling you to recognize some of the situations when you encounter them. It will also provide some important steps you can take to protect yourself against the possibility that a fraud artist might fleece you.

There is a list of resources where you can obtain more information about frauds and how to resist them. This is particularly valuable because, to paraphrase P.T. Barnum: "There's a new fraud every minute." Keeping up to date via the Internet is very helpful for this reason.

No book can provide 100 percent protection. Fraud artists are very imaginative and creative, with agile minds that adapt to the changing scene. This is why many are ahead of the law, avoiding prosecution by moving on to different locales and using different techniques to avoid the broken arm of the law. This highlights the need for you to be especially vigilant, and to develop a paranoid attitude. It's all right to think that they're out to get you, because they are!

Notes:

1. National Fraud Center, *Identity Theft: Authentication as a Solution*, pp. 4-5.
2. Blyth, Ashley E., "Quantifying Fraud is Hard," *Security Products*, June 2000, p. 8.

3. Pettinari, Cmdr. Dave, "The Basics of Investigating Credit Card Fraud on the Internet," *Police & Security News*, May/June 2000, p. 62.
4. National Fraud Center, *Identity Theft: Authentication as a Solution*, p. 5.

Chapter One
Organized Crime:
Stripping Away the Illusions

The image most people have of organized crime is a bunch of swarthy men with Italian surnames and dark suits running liquor and gambling rackets, and occasionally murdering their rivals. Movies such as *The Godfather* and others have fostered this image, which is an outdated stereotype. If we take the movies seriously, these organized crime types run around "making offers you can't refuse," or committing drive-by shootings with Tommy guns. Real organized crime today is vastly different from that image, and far more threatening because it's so insidious. It's far less violent than the movie stereotypes, and much more business-like, and often resembles legitimate business because

Movie stereotypes about organized crime are misleading. It is less violent, but more dangerous than the popular image, and it is not the monopoly of one nationality or ethnic group. Organized crime is insidious, because it crosses the line into legitimate business and is often not recognized as criminal activity.

Many dishonest business practices are nevertheless legal, such as the insurance industry and their mandatory auto insurance; the airline industry and their ability to hike fares and cram as many passengers as they can onto a plane without regard for their safety; motor vehicle theft and chop shops supplying parts to unsuspecting customers; advertising; you name it, it's here, and more.

it crosses the line into legitimate business. Also, organized crime is not the monopoly of one nationality or ethnic group.

The real danger is that organized crime today is largely unrecognized as criminal enterprise, even by law enforcement, which leaves organized criminals free to prey on unsuspecting citizens with almost no interference by police. Another reason is that organized crime is often several jumps ahead of the police, and law enforcement is constantly playing "catch-up." As we'll see in the chapter on credit card fraud, organized crime rings are very agile and very mobile, and take advantage of the fragmented nature of law enforcement.

Organized crime also includes "white-collar crime," most of which is over the line between legal and illegal. At times, white-collar crime is not even illegal. A lobbyist who makes a "campaign contribution" to a lawmaker is merely handing over a bribe. Likewise a corporation that pays a lawmaker's way on a "fact-finding trip" to a plush resort.

Organized crime also includes various types of street crime to support its activities. Car thieves supply "chop shops." Mailbox raiders procure checks for check forgery rings. Burglars often sell checks and credit cards they steal to organized rings. We'll study these in detail later.

The basic principle of organized crime is that it blends imperceptibly into legitimate business. A businessman who buys cut-rate materials without inquiring whether they might have been stolen is supporting organized crime. A business manager or owner who pays off a labor leader to avoid a strike is an active co-conspirator with organized crime. The organized crime leader sets up a legitimate business to "launder" money gained through illegal activities.

There are some common organized crime frauds that have become more remunerative today, partly because of technological advances and social changes. One is the office supply fraud, using several techniques.

The simplest is to bill a company for fictitious supplies or services. These scams often involve office consumables, such as copy machine toner, light bulbs, and cleaning supplies. The scammer depends on overworked and harried office workers not taking the time to check the origins of every invoice or to confirm that the product or service was actually delivered. This method seems to be more successful today because of corporate "downsizing," which often results in fewer staff to do the same amount of work.

The scammer may also ship merchandise that was never ordered, then bill the "customer." In some companies, the comptroller's office will pay any bill it can match with a receiving report. The Federal Trade Commission told the Senate Committee on Small Business that office supply fraud is a growing problem, and costs victims about $200 million annually.[1]

The FTC has worked to prosecute office supply fraud artists, in cooperation with other enforcement agencies. In December 1999, the FTC and the state of Illinois filed 14 cases against office supply fraud practitioners. Despite this, the problem continues to grow for the usual reasons: scammers are clever and agile, changing locations often, and thereby staying a step or two ahead of the law.

A variation of the fictitious bill technique is one used against consumers by some magazines. The publisher will send bills out to millions of people on a mailing list, hoping that a certain number of these people will think that they forgot that they'd ordered the magazines, and will pay the bill. Those who pay do receive their subscriptions. This keeps the publisher just on this side of the law, because he actually delivers what the customer paid for.

The best and most effective technique organized crime has to further its ends is co-opting the law and the machinery of government. This is perfectly legal, as we saw in the discussion of campaign contributions above. An example of the effects is the insurance industry.

Case Study: The Insurance Industry

Insurance is basically legalized gambling. When you buy an insurance policy, you're making a bet with the insurance company that something, such as fire, theft, or death, will happen to you. If you "win," the insurance company pays you the contracted sum of money. Insurance is also a protection racket. Traditional protection rackets intimidated individuals and businessmen into making regular payments to "protect" them against vandalism. A gangster would approach a store owner, for example, and inform him that his store was in a high-risk area, and that there was great danger of vandalism. The gang would, for a monetary consideration, undertake to "protect" him against vandals. If he paid, he'd have no problems. If he refused to pay, he'd find his window broken, or his store burned. Police, of course, took a dim view of this "protection" service, and would arrest gangsters for extortion. What if, however, it were possible to co-opt the police, and make them your enforcers? You'd have a captive clientele, who would be required by law to buy your protection. Let's look at how the insurance industry works.

You pay insurance company premiums to "protect" you against loss. An insurance company is a "legitimate" business. This means that if you don't buy fire insurance, the company's agents will not burn your house. If you don't have life insurance, they're not going to hire a hit man to kill you. They have other techniques, which are legal, because in one sense, insurance companies make the laws.

Years ago, automobile liability insurance was optional. However, the insurance companies lobbied legislators to pass laws making auto insurance mandatory. Today, you're required to have an insurance policy in force when you register your motor vehicle. In some states, the insurance company notifies the motor vehicle bureau if you allow your policy to lapse, and the bureau revokes your registration. If a police officer stops you and you don't have proof of insurance, he'll write you a ticket.

What's wrong with that? Well, there's a lot wrong with this set-up. For example, before 1983 auto insurance in Arizona was cheap and affordable. That was the year the Arizona legislature passed a law making liability insurance mandatory. With this step, Arizona motorists became captive clients. Without a choice, they saw their premiums ratcheting up every year. The same thing happened in every other state with mandatory auto insurance.

In some states, the mandatory insurance laws became very punitive. Mandatory insurance laws provide for high-risk drivers. These are motorists with histories of collisions who are more costly to insure. This also applies to those who have accumulated traffic tickets.

High-risk drivers have trouble obtaining auto insurance. For these, there is an "assigned risk pool," a program that distributes high-risk drivers to insurance companies on a rotating basis to insure. The insurance company, in consideration of the higher risk, is allowed to charge more, a surcharge that applies to high-risk drivers and can go up to at least twice the regular premium, depending on the individual's record. So far, this seems fair. However, the assigned risk pool is easy to abuse, and some insurance companies have done exactly that.

In New York, several years ago, drivers with clean records found their policies being canceled arbitrarily, thereby throwing them into the assigned risk pool. One provision of New York State law allowed insurance companies to refuse to insure any driver whose insurance had been canceled. They were forced to buy the same insurance at a higher price, in this case with a 50 percent surcharge. This was nothing more than a racket, with the backing of the government. The insurance companies took no risk, because they had the government, including the police, on their side. The police became the enforcers of this pernicious practice. There was nothing an individual could do to protest, except turn in his registration and sell his car.

Case Study:
The Airlines

Another example is the airline industry, which has a powerful lobby to influence legislators, and is "regulated" by the Federal Aviation Administration (FAA), staffed largely by former airline personnel. This is why the airline industry has a tremendous influence on the nature of the "regulations" it has to follow. Twenty years ago, the airline lobby was able to have the federal government "deregulate" airlines, so that they could pursue greater profits.

Profit is the name of the game. The more passengers you can cram into an airliner, the more profit you earn, even if it means installing thinner seats that offer less protection against impacts than traditional airline seats. Thinner seats allow cramming more people into a given space, and contribute to high profits.

Ever wonder why the airlines install only lap belts in passenger seats, while auto manufacturers are required by law to install shoulder harnesses? It's a proven fact that shoulder harnesses are safer, but airlines still use the less effective, and cheaper, lap belts. Cars today are required to have air bags, yet airlines do not install them, because they would cost more than belts, and would add to the thickness of each seat, reducing the number of people who could be crammed into a fuselage.

However, the pilots have large, sturdy seats and shoulder harnesses.

Military pilots have even more. Every military pilot and crewman has a shoulder harness, for a start. Military pilots also have parachutes. Parachutes are not new technology, because they've been around since the First World War. However, commercial airliners have none. The airlines don't provide them, using the excuse that passengers haven't been trained in their use. Of course, passengers haven't been trained in surviving 150-mile-per-hour crash landings, either. As for ejector seats, the airlines won't even discuss them.

Airlines have found that it's cheaper, in the short run, to ignore safety issues, because spending on safety cuts into the bottom line. An airline CEO holds office for only a few years, and if he can show high profits during his tenure, the board of directors is more likely to vote him a "golden parachute" on his retirement. After that, it's the next CEO's problem. Each CEO counts on the prospect that "It won't happen to me during my watch." Most are right, because they hold office only a few years.

Occasionally, events catch up to an airline. Pan American folded after the Lockerbie disaster. Granted, this was the result of a terrorist bomb, but Pan American had widely advertised its security measures. When terrorists were still able to place a bomb on board the airliner, the result was a flurry of lawsuits that sunk the airline.

Case Study: Chop Shops

Motor vehicle theft is a serious problem in the United States, and ranges from adolescents who steal a car for a spree of "joy-riding" to well-organized rings that steal cars in order to satisfy the needs of their customers. Some car theft rings steal cars, "launder" them to provide new titles and registrations, and sell them to buyers who may or may not know that the cars have been stolen. Another type of organized crime related to motor vehicles is the "chop shop," a perfect example of how an illegal enterprise supplies legal businesses. Chop shops exist because people today keep their cars longer than they did years ago, given the price of new cars.

Factory replacement parts are expensive, and many repair shops persuade their customers that parts salvaged from wrecked cars are inexpensive replacements. A slightly used engine from a wrecking yard costs a fraction of the price of a factory engine. A new hood or fender costs much more if purchased from a dealer than an undamaged one salvaged from a used or wrecked car. This is also true for many other parts, such as transmissions, differentials, and doors.

Not all such "recycled" parts come from wrecks. The chop shop receives vehicles from car theft rings and cuts them up for spare parts, which it sells to repair shops and auto body shops. The chop shop cycle is a perfect example of how a criminal enterprise blends in with legitimate business. The owner of a repair shop may or may not know that the parts he buys from a wrecking yard come from stolen vehicles. He may not even care. Almost certainly his customers don't know.

The same cycle, from criminal enterprise to legitimate business, is true for many other industries. The truck-hijacking ring sells its stolen TVs, stereos, and VCRs to a network of distributors, which in turn resells them to legitimate dealers, often in another part of the country. The retail customer who buys a TV from a "discount" house doesn't truly know its origin, and in buying the bargain unwittingly supports organized crime.

We see other business activities that border on organized crime, remaining just this side of the fine dividing line. Advertising is a conspicuous example. The advertised low price of a computer or cellular phone is in large type, while the fine print at the bottom of the ad states conditions, such as requiring a three-year subscription to an Internet Service Provider or a cellular phone service to obtain the promised rebate.

One customer signed up for a VISA card under a plan that promised "no annual fee." However, when he received his first bill, a $75 annual fee was included. He had signed without reading the fine print.[2] This is not an accident. Advertisements contain bold print designed to make the offer attractive. The contract contains fine print designed to be hard to understand and time consuming to read. Marketers know that this will deter many customers from thoroughly reading the contract they sign, and when the customer eventually discovers that he's signed a contract different from the advertising promise, he won't have a leg to stand on.[3]

Another type of organized crime that operates just this side of the dividing line involves "oversubscribing." This means signing up more customers than the business can handle, then declaring bankruptcy and making off with the profits. During the 1970s many "health clubs" sprang up around the country. Some offered "lifetime" memberships at absurdly low prices. Customers who accepted these offers found that when they tried to collect on the services offered, the parking lots were full and the facilities were jammed. Many of these health clubs closed after one or two years, leaving their life members high and dry.

The same thing happened with various Internet Service Providers. America Online was the first to offer unlimited online time, and it captured a lot of customers very quickly. Others immediately followed to remain competitive, and customers found that when they tried to connect, they usually received busy signals. This led to lawsuits by several state attorney generals, and the situation has improved.

Today, we see the same occurring with cell-phone providers. Some offer package deals with thousands of minutes a month at an unrealistically low price. Customers find that they get busy signals when they try to connect and they have great difficulty obtaining the promised airtime.

From all this we see that organized crime is more than rings of dope dealers and distributors, chop shops, and hijacking rings. Each illegal enterprise has its network of supporters, and some legitimate businesses and industries are powerful enough to write their own laws. Organized crime is tightly woven into the fabric of our economy, and there's little hope of extirpating it.

Notes:

1. Press release: Federal Trade Commission, Washington, D.C., March 28, 2000.
2. Mayer, Caroline E., "Big Promises Backed Up by Small Print," *The Sunday Journal*, June 18, 2000, p. C1.
3. *Ibid.*, p. C2.

Chapter Two
Telephone Scams

Your telephone rings and a pleasant, friendly voice tells you:

"This is the XYZ Credit Card Verification Service and we're verifying credit card accounts for your protection. Please read me your credit card numbers and their expiration dates so that we may enter them into our computer to prevent unauthorized use."

If you believe this scam artist, you'll soon find many charges against your credit card account, because you'll have unwittingly given away the family jewels. No credit card company telephones clients to ask for their credit card numbers and expiration dates, as they already have this information on file.

> Never give any personal information to anyone who calls you up claiming to be a credit card verification service, bank officer, police, or other authorities.
>
> Do not give out:
>
> ■ Credit card numbers
> ■ Expiration dates
> ■ Social Security numbers
> ■ Bank account numbers
>
> Watch out for "boiler room calls" offering you:
>
> ■ Real estate
> ■ Travel packages
> ■ Push polls
> ■ Anything that sounds to good to be true.

Other fraud artists pose as bank officers, police officers, and other authorities to obtain this information from victims. They ask for card numbers, Social Security numbers, bank account numbers, and other identifying information under various pretexts. All of these are scams, because a legitimate bank or credit card officer will never telephone to ask for account numbers.

The fraud artist persuades an individual to provide this information, and then uses the number and expiration date to make purchases by telephone and over the Internet, and the charges appear on the customer's bill. This racket requires fast work, before the individual realizes he's been victimized and has his card deactivated. Typically, the racket operates out of a "boiler room," a rented office with many telephone lines, and the victims are usually out-of-state credit card holders to make it more difficult for police to investigate and prosecute. One group of scam artists makes the telephone calls to obtain card numbers, and another group uses them to make purchases.

The telephone makes it easy for fraud artists to victimize gullible people because the contact is impersonal and remote. A perfect example is real estate fraud, in which a telescammer persuades victims to buy worthless property, knowing that the victim cannot examine the land over the phone, but must take the scammer's word that the property is valuable and will quickly accrue in value.[1] Travel scams are flourishing because fraud artists have discovered that they can sell bogus travel packages over the telephone. The basic technique is to offer a very attractive price for the package, an "offer you can't refuse." If the offer is a total fraud, you'll be asked for a "processing fee" up front, or if you have to provide a credit card number to pay for the package, the scammer can make off with your money and leave you waiting for your tickets to arrive.[2]

Even "legitimate" travel agencies sometimes take advantage of their clients by booking them on "bargain" tours without telling them all of the conditions. The reason is that many people will assume that a "package deal" covers all of the expenses. Not so. The sales representative may tell you that one price will cover the entire tour, but once you're on the tour, you find that you have to pay for meals, bus fares, port taxes, and many other miscellaneous fees.

Boiler Rooms

These boiler room scammers use several techniques to make them harder to trace. Operating across state lines is the basic technique, because law enforcement agencies have limited jurisdictions, and are reluctant to investigate crimes that take place in other locales. Boiler room operators also use mobility to evade prosecution. They rent offices on short-term leases, fill them with rented furniture, and change locations regularly to stay ahead of the law.

Frequent change of location makes them almost impossible to prosecute. Before a law enforcement agency can gather enough evidence and bring it to the local prosecutor, or arrange cooperation with a prosecutor who has jurisdiction where the boiler room is located, the scam artists have closed shop and set up their operation in another state. This mobility makes them almost immune to effective prosecution.

Another technique is to use electronic trickery to make them harder to locate, even with Caller ID. Caller ID devices are available in electronic stores. There are also electronic devices that block your phone from providing identifying information, and these are favorites of scam artists. The incoming call appears as "OUT OF AREA" on your Caller ID box, so that you have no idea of its point of origin.

There is a service offered to certain businesses by the telephone company to dodge "Caller ID." Normal unlisted numbers appear on Caller ID as "BLOCKED CALL" or "PRIVATE CALL." This service, which is closely held, is available only to newspapers, telemarketers, and other businesses who want to disguise the origin of calls they make without tipping the Caller ID owner that it is a blocked call. Instead, the legend on the Caller ID box reads "OUT OF AREA," as if the call originated in a remote location. In fact, the caller may be as close as a mile away. In an effort to pin down this type of service, the author made several calls to the telephone company and discovered that the service representatives deny that such a service exists.

If you receive a fraudulent telephone call and bring a complaint to the police, you can't even tell the officers from where the call originated. "Tracing" the call doesn't work, because the telephone company will not give out this information except to a police agency, and sometimes requires a court order. An individual cannot obtain the origin of such a call. By the time a law enforcement agency can pursue the case, the boiler room has moved.

Another part of this problem is the telephone company, which takes the position that it only rents telephone lines, and is not responsible for any misuse. This is in sharp contrast to the policy of another medium, the U.S. Postal Service. There are laws against using the U.S. Mail for fraud, and there is a staff of Postal Inspectors which investigates mail fraud. The telephone company also employs security officers, but their effort is against people who try to defraud the telephone company, not against scam artists who defraud individuals who faithfully pay their phone bills.

Another telephone scam is the "push poll," a spurious telephone poll used by some candidates to spread negative information about their opponents before an election. The pollster, under the guise of soliciting your opinion, asks you loaded questions designed to influence the way you vote.

One example is: "Candidate Smith is pro-abortion. Will this cause you not to vote for him in the next election?"

Another is: "District Attorney Smith's record of convictions is lower than the national average. Will you still vote for him?"

Yet another is: "Were you aware that most of Smith's campaign contributions came from labor unions? Are you in favor of this type of fund-raising?"

All of these are designed to influence your vote, not to solicit your opinion, although they are cleverly worded to sound like legitimate polling questions. This practice is not, strictly speaking, illegal, although many would consider it unethical because of the deception involved.

If you receive a call from someone obviously conducting a push poll, one way to cope is to immediately notify the opponent's campaign staff to alert them of the tactic being used against their candidate. Begin by asking for the caller's name and telephone number so that you can provide some hard information. The caller may or may not provide his real name and telephone number, but write it down anyway. The other candidate will have some ammunition to use if the name and number turn out to be as spurious as the questions.

Calling Card Scams

If you have a telephone calling card, guard it as carefully as you would a credit card. However, this isn't total protection. Many telephone calling cards require that you punch in the card number whenever you make a call on it. This isn't a problem if you use the card to pay for a long-distance call from a friend's telephone or the office of a business contact. However, if you make a call from a public phone, you're vulnerable to a "shoulder surfer," a scam artist who frequents airports, railroad stations, and other places where he can observe travelers using their calling cards to place calls. In a crowded airport, the shoulder surfer may do exactly what the name implies, peering over your shoulder to see the numbers you punch in on the dial pad. He may also be at a table on a balcony coffee shop, watching the phone booth below with a telescope. The most sophisticated surfers use a camcorder, zooming in on people at public telephones, thereby getting a photographic record they can study at leisure. This practice is insidious because you can have your calling card number stolen without being aware of it until you receive a huge bill from your telephone company.[3]

There are a couple of defenses against surfers. One is to obtain a calling card with a magnetic strip to allow you to swipe it through a card reader slot on the public phone. However, many public telephones don't have a card reader, and you still have to punch in the number manually, leaving you vulnerable to anyone watching.

The other, and better, way to defend yourself against this type of scam is to use prepaid calling cards that you can buy in drugstores, supermarkets, and convenience stores. Buy a 30-minute or 60-minute card, so that even if someone lifts your number or you lose the card, nobody can run up an astronomical phone bill for you. The most you can lose is the amount you've paid for the card.

Telephones can be very helpful, but they can also bring many problems for the unwary. You have to know your way around modern technology for your own protection.

Notes:

1. Engel, Peter H., *SCAM!,* New York, St. Martin's Press, 1996, pp. 19-20.
2. *Ibid.,* pp. 25-26.
3. *Ibid.,* pp. 69-70.

Chapter Three
Cellular Phones

During the last decade a new type of fraud appeared, based upon fraudulent use of cellular phone accounts. Unlike the old technology of physically tapping in to a landline telephone's wires to make phone calls, this new scheme requires no physical connection.

Every cell phone emits its identification number constantly when turned on, to identify itself to the nearest station to receive incoming calls. The scam artist uses a special receiver to pluck your account number from the air. Typically, he'll set up opera-

A new type of fraud takes advantage of the fact that every cell phone broadcasts its identification number when turned on. A scam artist can use a special receiver to get the number, with which he can make long-distance calls charged to your account.

The only defense against this is to leave your cell phone turned off, except when you make a call. No one can call you, but with voice messaging you don't have to miss calls. And, of course, it's safer to avoid making any phone calls while you're driving.

tion near a busy intersection, knowing that of the many people driving through, a certain number will have their cell phones turned on. You don't have to be talking on your phone for him to get your number. He then programs your account number into a chip (known as an "e-prom") designed to fit into a cell phone, and begins to make long-distance calls charged to your account.

Unfortunately, there is no easy defense against this type of scam. When you turn on your cell phone, there is no way to tell if anyone besides the cell phone service provider is picking up your transmissions. If you leave it on all day to receive incoming calls, you're vulnerable to interception every moment.

There is a passive defense available, though. Simply leave your cell phone turned off except for when you initiate a call. Nobody will be able to reach you, but with voice messaging you won't miss calls. You can check your voice mailbox periodically to find out who's called you.

This passive defense covers you in several ways. First, it minimizes your time on the air, greatly reducing the chances of a scammer intercepting your account number. This also practically eliminates junk calls. Telemarketers don't care if they run up your charges while they try to sell you something, and it can be both annoying and expensive to answer your cell phone to discover that it's merely a salesman wasting your time.

Finally, it's safer if you're driving. While some people think it's cool to hold a cell phone in one hand while driving with the other, it's also dangerous, especially in city traffic. If you keep your phone turned off, you won't risk being distracted by an incoming call. Naturally, you'll also want to pull into a parking lot if there's an urgent call you have to make.

Telephone technology is more complex than before, because of the wide variety of equipment available, especially in the wireless field. Telephone use also requires more sophistication because of cultural changes, and you have to keep up with these to make the telephone your servant instead of your persecutor.

Chapter Four
Romance and Personal Scams

Today's hurried pace of living has resulted in both a deterioration of personal relationships and several high-tech substitutes for them. Some people live their lives online, frequenting chat rooms and finding emotional gratification in them. Occasionally, inhabitants of chat rooms seek personal contact with other chatters. Others seek romance through Internet dating services, personal ads, and chat rooms for people of similar interests. Often, this is futile, because these media are perfect hunting grounds for scammers.

Having a realistic idea of what to expect is an important step, even if you're not

Romance phone lines, chat rooms, Internet meeting places, and singles publications are all rife with fraud.

Romance phone lines charge you by the minute, waste your time, and keep you on the line as long as possible. And there's no guarantee you'll get any response to your message.

Individuals who place romance ads also engage in deception, such as falsely describing themselves or hiding important information.

Beyond this, some advertisers have hidden agendas, some of which can be predatory or dangerous. Hidden agendas can include the married person seeking an illicit affair or the person juggling more than one relationship. Some people are gold diggers, seeking to marry and divorce for money. Others are "game players" of one kind or another. Be very cautious if you use these services.

victimized by a scammer. Are you looking for "Mr. Right" or "Miss Perfect?" Think again:

"Miss Perfect never comes, second choice rejects you, third choice marries you and takes half of everything you own in the divorce, so you have to settle for fourth choice."

However, we're not going to get into the intricacies of defining and setting up a personal romance here, because the purpose of this book is to discuss scammers. There is a lot of fraud and deception in romance ads, chat rooms, and Internet meeting places. These also exist in other media, such as singles' publications and "romance" newspaper ads as well. These may be frauds for financial gain, or simple lies by people who want to conceal their deficiencies to appeal to potential romantic contacts. What you "see" is often not what you get.

There are individual scams, and organized scams. We're going to examine how people deceive each other through these media, and how at times the media themselves engage in legal, but deceptive, practices to earn money off the lonely. Let's look at these first.

Romance Lines

This type of telephone scam is perfectly legal, although to many of us it would appear illegitimate, or at least deceptive. Many newspapers and magazines feature "romance" columns, with personal ads placed by single people. Previous practice was that anyone answering the ad had to address a written reply to a romance box number at the publication's address, enclosing a fee of a dollar or two. The amount that one could spend was strictly defined and limited. The introduction of the 900-number changed all that.

Today, typically there is no charge for placing the ad. Replying via phone is expensive if the publication has a voice-mail service. You dial a 900-number, punch in the number of the ad, and the meter starts running. The usual charge is two or more dollars per minute, but don't expect to get away with two bucks a call. The fine print at the bottom of the romance column explicitly lists the per-minute charge for calling the number, thereby taking the publication off the hook. What the fine print doesn't tell you is how the system will waste your time, keeping you running up the meter as long as possible. The businessmen who operate these voice-mail companies have well-calculated ways to keep you on the line to increase their return from each call.

You first hear an introductory taped message, giving you basic instructions regarding which buttons to push, then the service allows you to choose which numbers you wish to contact. You'll probably have to listen to a recorded message by the person who placed the ad, which means it's practically impossible to limit the call to just leaving your name and number. Some services allow recording these advertisers' messages at no charge, because they make their money from the replies. This encourages the person who placed the ad to be long-winded. It's not costing him or her anything, although it does cost the listener two or more dollars per minute to listen.

Once you've listened to the verbal message, you can record your own. Because you're being charged by the minute and the meter is running, you're likely to keep it short, telling a bit about yourself and leaving your name and phone number.

After this, you know that you've gotten your reply into the advertiser's voice-mailbox, but this doesn't mean that you'll get as speedy a return call, or even guarantee that you'll get a reply at all. The only guarantee is that the charge will appear on next month's phone bill! Yet, this is perfectly legal.

Perhaps the worst part is that you have no assurance that the ad was real. It may have been run by the publisher just to attract calls to the 900-number.

This isn't the only hazard involved in answering romance ads. There are individual deceptions as well. Anyone with experience answering such ads will tell you that many advertisers lie. A man who lists his age as 65 will sometimes appear to be closer to 75 or 85. A woman who states that she has a "voluptuous" figure is sometimes merely fat. People will overstate their good points and conceal their deficiencies. An ex-convict will certainly not disclose this in his ad. A woman with a vicious temper will try to appear patient and loving.[1]

The main hazard is that the other person may have a hidden agenda, criminal or emotional, and you have to be alert for danger signs. Let's look at one conspicuous example:

> "WANTING IT ALL! Very attractive 50's, successful DWPF with incredibly active life filled with fun, friends and adventures, would like to share in LTR with man secure enough to seek a companion in his own age group and who has at least a job and a clue! Needy, unemployed, impotent, commitment-phobics need not respond. Extra points for own teeth and hair. Sense of humor a MUST."

The clues were in the ad, but the man who replied did not appreciate their hidden meaning. First, the ad was very negative, and implied a pejorative view of men. This woman, who worked as a clinical psychologist and stated she did not want a "commitment-phobic" person, was actually describing herself. The very obvious clue was in the phrase "incredibly active life filled with fun, friends and adventures." With such a busy life, she wasn't interested in an LTR, and this became clear when they met. She told him that she planned to move to Czechoslovakia within six months. That, of course, made it almost impossible for any man to maintain a relationship with her.

Game Playing

Reading personal ads, we run across the phrase "game-playing" again and again. Some advertisers state clearly in their ads that they do not want "game-players." At this point, it's worth looking closely at game playing and game players, define them clearly, and list some of the games these people play.

For our purpose, it's enough to begin by defining a "game-player" as a person who is dishonest, following a hidden agenda, leading the other person on while playing by different rules. A "game" can be simple, such as lying about one's age or marital status, or it can be more complex and subtle, such as jockeying for control.

It's a given that many people have hidden agendas. Some agendas are innocuous, while others are predatory and danger-ous. What all game-players have in common is that they're go-ing to be intellectually or emotionally dishonest with you. These categories overlap, as some involved in the singles search have more than one deficiency.

The Liar

This is perhaps the most common type, purposely misstating his qualifications by an outright misstatement or a lie by omis-sion. The dishonest person conceals facts about himself, his history, or his motives. He may conceal the fact that he's mar-ried, on parole, or unemployed. A tip-off is the person who continues to refuse to provide his address.

Age is a common characteristic to misrepresent. The man who replied to Kay's ad said he was 65-years-old, not much older than Kay. When she met him for coffee, he was so de-crepit that he appeared to be closer to 85.

There are several ways of lying about age. Some send pho-tographs of themselves, which may not be recent. One man found that the woman who replied to his ad sent a photo that had to be at least ten years old.

Another type of liar is the married person (legal or common-law) seeking an affair without letting the other party know of the previous commitment. A few married people will seek an affair with full informed consent of the other party, although they'll keep it from the spouse.

The subtler liar, the game-player, doesn't conceal overt facts, but mis-states his motives. An excellent example is the liar who replies to an ad that states "Long-Term Relationship." The liar will not admit that he only wants a quickie, and intends to have relationships with others at the same time.

Although we'll get into lie detection later, take warning that it's not as easy to spot a liar as some people think. Body language, linguistics, and other methods aren't as reliable as they've been touted, because some people are very skilled and practiced liars who have all of their moves and stories well-rehearsed.

The Hidden Agenda

This may be the married person seeking an illicit affair or the person juggling more than one relationship at a time. In both cases, there will be a reluctance to provide information that can help you find or trace him. Another type of hidden agenda is the free-dinner date.

The Dinner Date

This is usually a woman who places or answers an ad, feigning interest in the man, and who will accept a date for dinner if he pays for it. This game-player knows that many men try to impress a woman by taking her to an expensive restaurant on the first date. After eating the free meal, she'll abruptly drop him, telling him they have nothing in common, or simply not return his phone calls. One possible warning sign is if the woman shows a lack of interest in a "coffee-only" date. A good way to guard against this ploy is to make it a hard and fast rule never to go for anything more expensive than a coffee-only first date.

The Asset Collector

There is a small minority of women (a few men play this game, too) whose only means of support is marrying affluent men, then enriching themselves by taking half their assets in the subsequent divorce. With most states now following "community property" laws, the couple's assets are divided between the two upon dissolution of the marriage, and in most cases regardless of who earned them. In some states, only assets earned during the marriage are subject to this 50-50 split, while in others all of the properties are divided right down the middle.

This points up the importance of economic parity in a relationship. If one party is significantly more affluent than the other, it casts doubt regarding the less affluent person's motives: "Is it love, or is it money?" The only way to be sure is to begin relationships only with someone of the same socio-economic background.

The Never Married

As we've seen, some people are afraid of getting into a relationship or of getting married. The person who reaches age 30 or 40 without having been married may be a problem personality, afraid of commitments. Experience shows that such people not only lie to others, but lie to themselves as well. Instead of squarely facing their fear of becoming seriously involved with someone else, they pretend that they haven't met anyone who is up to their standards. In fact, their standards are impossibly high, and this posturing saves them from having to consider any other person for a long-term relationship.

The other possibility is that such people are so undesirable that nobody would want a relationship with them, and they've never been asked to marry. If this is the case, the problem will appear quickly.

The Predator

This type also has a hidden agenda, often not at all obvious. This may be simply a collector, a rapist, or a game-player who gets his thrills by inducing people to waste their time. This can involve making dates and blowing them off, or leading the other party to think that there's a serious prospect, then suddenly withdrawing.

The Emotional Game-Player

There are many types of game-players, some of whom get their thrills by playing games to frustrate the other person or find another way to hurt the other person emotionally. These are a constant threat, because they carefully hide their motives at the outset, instead appearing very charming and interesting at first.

Jane agreed to meet a couple of men who had replied to her ad for coffee, although she had admitted to a friend that she wasn't interested in a relationship. Her purpose was merely to satisfy her curiosity regarding what type of men would answer her ad. In effect, she was just wasting these men's time, because her agenda was very different from theirs.

She had also confided that she knew how to hurt men by having sex with them once, and then refusing all other sexual contacts. It became obvious that Jane was carrying a lot of emotional baggage, and anyone starting on a relationship with her would be hugging a time bomb.

The Toe Dipper

This person isn't willing to commit to a relationship, although he may reply to ads that specify "LTR." This type has been so hurt, and has not yet recovered from a previous relationship, that he's afraid to become involved again. There may also be deeper personal reasons, such as an unwillingness to accept the responsibility that goes with a long-term relationship. He'll answer an ad, but back off quickly if the other person appears at all serious.

The Collector

The collector is typically male, although females playing this game are not unknown. The purpose is to make as many sexual conquests as possible. The collector comes on strong, is very attentive and ardent, but after a sexual experience loses interest. Some collectors will use aliases, to prevent former partners from tracing and pursuing them. A sure tip-off is the person who persistently refuses to provide a telephone number or address. This is incontrovertible evidence that this person has something significant to hide.

Vinnie was a very suave and skilled collector who deserved the Oscar for the acting proficiency he displayed. Married and with four children, he did not wear a wedding ring, and spent a good deal of time trolling for attractive young women. He used an alias to make it hard for a woman to trace him to his home. His modus operandi was to find a woman, charm her, have sex with her, and then drop her. He would boast to his business associates that his formula was the "Four F's: Find 'em, Feel 'em, Fuck 'em, and Forget 'em."

The Heartbreaker

The heartbreaker is typically a woman angry at men, and who intends to make men pay for injustices that a man may have inflicted on her in the long ago. She will be very sweet and accommodating, until she sees that the man has become emotionally attached to her. At that point, she'll drop him abruptly and coldly.

The "Control Person"

The "control freak" can be male or female, and the purpose is always to dominate the relationship. There are different ways of exercising control: some are crude, while others are more subtle.

Jean was a control freak, and exercised control by being very demanding. She insisted that a man was to dress up for any date with her, pick her up at her home, always open doors for her, and even follow the protocol of walking her to her door and kissing her good night after a date. She became offended if the man did not follow her protocol exactly.

Gina stated at the outset that she spent a lot of time on her job and doing volunteer work after hours, and would have limited time for a relationship. The purpose was to make the man wait for her convenience, and she would ration out her time to him at a pace she controlled. Fortunately, she was obvious about this, providing any aspiring male fair warning.

The male control freak can be very demanding, expecting the woman to be available for him any time he wishes, and demanding an explanation of any time she spends doing something else. Again, this type of control freak exposes his agenda early in the relationship.

Passive-Aggressive

The term "passive-aggressive" comes from the field of psychology, where it denotes someone who displays aggression by passive resistance. Being passive-aggressive is not so much a game as an attitude, expressing hostility towards the other person. It can take many forms:

- Being repeatedly late and offering excuses.
- Forgetting to call or keep in touch.
- Not returning phone calls.
- Not being ready on time.
- Not showing up for a date.

These are some simple ways of showing passive aggression. At times, it can become ridiculous indeed:

"What's the time, dear?"

"Oh, I don't know."

"But you have a watch on your wrist."

"Yes, but I can't be bothered looking."

When a dialog deteriorates to this point, it's best for the other party to split and not look back.

More complex and subtle kinds of passive-aggression are common. Most involve complaints of illness or discomfort.

Judy, who described herself as "eccentric," had a long list of complaints that made life hard for her partners:

- Car seats were uncomfortable, so she could not go on long road trips. When she did, she always brought a pillow or two, and constantly shifted and fidgeted in her seat.
- She stated that she had ADD, Attention Deficit Disorder, so she could not watch a movie or TV program for any length of time.
- She could not understand the instructions for setting the time on her stereo player's clock, and asked her partner to do it for her.
- She had to watch her food intake, and ate only small portions. This made it awkward to take her to a restaurant, as did her propensity to complain about the way restaurant food was prepared. In one instance, she sent the dish back, and ordered another selection, because she didn't like the way it had been prepared.

- She was too restless to sleep in the same bed with another person.
- Sex was painful for her.
- She was sensitive to heat, and could not go outside much during the warm season.
- Because of her sensitivity to heat, she would not have sex from the late spring to early fall.

What made it clear that this was game-playing and not true disability was that her disorders were very selective. When one of her partners took her on an expensive weekend away from home, she was somehow able to ride for several hours on the road, and even insisted on driving for most of the return trip. Despite her claimed ADD, Judy managed to keep her attention on the road for several hours and proved to be a skilled driver. She also managed to eat the meals with gusto, and share a king-size bed with her partner.

The "Rules" Player

A recent book written by two women for women, advocates playing a very dishonest game with men to keep them guessing and off-balance, and to keep the woman firmly in control of all aspects of the relationship. This is a variation of the "control" game. Among the "rules" laid out are:

- Don't accept any date for the weekend if the man calls later than Wednesday.
- Don't return all of his phone calls.
- Disconnect the answering machine to keep him further off balance.

This is very dangerous advice, for an obvious reason. Women cannot afford to play games because there are more women out there than men. A man who suspects that a woman is playing games can simply look elsewhere.

The Moocher

This type is often impecunious, and may begin by asking for money or for a ride. At times, this can lead to ridiculous situations. When Kathy met the man who'd replied to her ad, he asked her for a lift to his parole officer's bureau. Another man also did not have a car, and asked for transportation to the food stamp office.

There are several types of moochers, and ironically some advertisers actively seek out certain types because they fill a need. The older widow who wants a "boy-toy" is perfectly willing to support a young man who provides her with satisfying sex. Her viewpoint is that "A hard man is good to find."

Also, we have the traditional and stereotypical "sugar daddy" who is willing to exchange support for sex. Let's note here that seeking younger partners is not limited to mainstream heterosexuals. Some people who are into same-sex contacts and other unusual forms of sexual expression also want young flesh, and are willing to pay for it.

The Negotiator

This uncommon type can be annoying to deal with, but isn't dangerous. The negotiator never accepts a proposal as given, but wants to negotiate changes. If, for example, you ask for a Sunday morning date, you'll find out that she attends church each Sunday morning. If you want to meet at a certain place, this isn't convenient, and she'll come back at you with another location.

The negotiator is hard to spot at first because all of the objections and counter-proposals appear reasonable. The tip-off is the pattern, as you notice that the other person never, or almost never, accepts a date in the way you suggest it. There's always a counter-proposal, which can become annoying because it's difficult to deal with someone who never travels in a straight line.

There are two ways to deal with the negotiator. The first is to reply that the suggested modification in plans is impossible for you, giving a good reason why. The second is the all-or-nothing proposal, one that leaves the negotiator no choice but to take it or leave it. An example is asking the negotiator to accompany you to a party held by someone else, at a specific day and time. It'll be clear that negotiating with you to change the date or time will be useless. Another is a date for a sports event or a concert. The negotiator cannot contact the sports team or concert performers and ask them to change their schedule for his convenience.

The negotiator, while annoying, isn't as dangerous as the last two types.

The Blackmailer

This criminal seeks to obtain documentary evidence that he can use to extract money from his victims. One blackmail ring that had placed personal ads in homosexual publications used Albuquerque, New Mexico, as a base of operations. Members of the ring would seek out sexual contacts with bisexual married men who obviously had something to hide, making them vulnerable. One ring member would have sex with the victim while another operated a hidden camcorder. The tape would serve as a handle for blackmail.

The Prison Inmate

He is undesirable for obvious reasons, and is very easy to spot because his address includes a long serial number after his name. The prisoner usually wants someone to visit him, bring food and money, and at times even to participate in an inmate scam, such as cashing forged money orders. A short-timer may want someone to provide for him upon release, promising love and affection in return. It's good to keep in mind that incarcerated felons are by nature con artists, and it's very risky to trust them. This is why some singles and offbeat sex publications include a warning at the beginning of each classified ad section:

"Don't be a victim. Some ads are invitations to financial scams or other frauds. Beware of anyone requesting financial favors or other 'help.' "

Fortunately, few prison inmates have access to the Internet. This means you're less likely to meet such a person in a chat room.

Early detection is the key to preventing harm from these various undesirable types. Most are dangerous only to your mental well-being. Only a few, such as blackmailers and prison inmates, pose greater threats.

Notes:

1. Engel, Peter H., *SCAM!*, New York, St. Martin's Press, 1996, pp. 126-127.

Chapter Five
Credit Card Fraud

Unless you're a hermit who lives in a cave, chances are that you've received many "pre-approved" credit card offers in the mail. Credit card providers are very aggressive in their blandishments, so much that a federal law came about to protect consumers against the worst abuses. Before this law, credit card companies could send out credit cards and activate an account without obtaining the customer's agreement, and even impose "service charges" if the customer did not use the card sent him. The dangers were obvious. Anyone raiding your mailbox could lift your new credit card and begin running up charges against your account.

Mailbox raiders may steal applications for credit cards, then fill out the agreement with your name, but a different address. When they receive the card, they run up charges in your name.

Another way scammers can get your credit card number and expiration date is with a "skimmer," a small, battery-operated version of the device used to read credit cards in stores. The only sure defense against a skimmer is to never let your credit card out of your sight. That will also protect you from the dishonest waiter or store clerk who might simply write down the name, number and expiration date on your credit card.

If you think your credit card has been compromised, call your provider at once.

Another variant on this theme is the outright fake invoice. The scam artist mails out cheaply printed notices designed to look as if they've been printed en masse by a computer. The form has your name and address on it, and informs you that you've been "pre-approved" for a credit card. All you have to do is send in $29.95 by the date listed. The notice continues with a threat: "Failure to do so may result in termination of your eligibility."

Today, the picture is still as dangerous, but it's changed somewhat. Credit card providers send applications, not cards, and you have to sign an agreement to receive the card. However, this still leaves you open to mailbox raiders, who can fill out the agreement in your name, but provide a different address. When they receive the card, they begin running up charges for which you'll eventually be billed.

Obviously you don't want to be victimized, and one way to stop this is never to accept any such offer. Also, keep an eye on your mailbox to prevent mail theft. The most secure way of safeguarding your mail is to use a post office box or a private mail drop.

There is yet another way for scammers to get your card number and expiration date. A device known as a "skimmer" records the data from the magnetic stripe when your card is slipped through its slot. This is the same device that a card reader at a store uses, but in this case it's a small, battery-operated device that a dishonest waiter or other person can use to obtain numbers for other members of his ring. The skimmer also reads the encrypted verification code that confirms the card's validity. The scam artists then upload your number and other data into a computer connected to an "encoder," which produces a new card with your data on its magnetic stripe. Members of the ring then use the forgeries to make purchases and charge them to your account.[1]

The only sure defense against a skimmer is never to let your credit card out of your sight. Make your purchases where you keep control of your credit card at all times. This isn't as hard as it seems. Supermarkets have point-of-sale terminals where you swipe your card through the card reader to pay for your purchases. Gas stations allow you to swipe the card through a card reader at the pump. Your card is never out of your hands. In other situations, watch the clerk every moment, and avoid buying anything where the clerk takes the card into a back room to produce a credit card slip. Instead, pay cash, and save yourself the risk.

There's worse news: A fraud artist doesn't even need high-tech devices to glean your credit card number. If you let your credit card out of your sight, a dishonest waiter or store clerk can simply copy the name, number, and expiration date. That's all a scammer needs to place telephone orders, using your credit card as payment. The insidious nature of this fraud is that you still have your credit card, and won't be aware that someone's charging purchases to your account until you receive your next statement.

This old scam is alive and well today. The U.S. Secret Service obtained a search warrant for an Albuquerque, New Mexico, restaurant after five customers had reported fraudulent charges on their credit card accounts. The suspects, all employees of the restaurant, had bought clothing, electronic equipment, shoes, and collector's edition quarters.[2]

Some credit card scammers are more aggressive. They hire burglars to break into homes to steal the victim's financial paperwork. They're not interested in TVs and VCRs, only the documents that allow them to take over the victim's financial identity and make fraudulent purchases. This is a new trend, and it's accelerating.[3]

One reason the credit card fraud problem is worse today is that a scam artist can make purchases over the Internet. This means that he does not have to show his face anywhere, and can gain access to Internet merchants through almost any telephone line. This makes it much harder for police to track fraud artists.

If you think your credit card has been compromised, call your provider immediately. With today's technology, it's possible to deactivate it within seconds, making further use impossible.

How Credit Card Providers Screw You

Illegal fraud artists are not the only dangers you face if you have a credit card. Many people find themselves flooded with credit card applications offering incredibly low rates. If they sign up, they soon find that the fine print states that the low rate is in effect for only a few months, and that thereafter the interest rate will be sky-high like the others.

It has become a source of annoyance to credit card providers that some of us pay off our credit card bills entirely as soon as they come due. This means that they can't charge us any interest. There are at least two ways of coping with this problem. One is to sneak in a "service charge" every now and then, knowing that most people do not scrutinize their credit card bills as carefully as they should and will pay the extra charge without questioning it. The other way is simply to skip sending out a bill one month. The credit card account holder may not notice, and next month his bill contains a month's interest on the unpaid balance. If he complains, he'll simply be told that maybe the post office "lost" his bill.

The way to defeat these little tricks is to be aware of them, and to monitor your credit card statements very carefully. Scan each item on the bill to make sure there are no extra charges sneaked in while you weren't looking. The other way is to scan your checkbook register each month, just to make sure you covered credit card bills that month. That will avoid your being charged extra interest by unscrupulous credit card providers.

Notes:

1. Shannon, Elaine, "A New Credit Card Scam," *Time*, June 5, 2000, pp. 54-55.
2. Contreras, Guillermo, "Eatery Investigated In Credit Card Fraud," *Albuquerque Journal*, June 8, 2000, p. 1.
3. Stiger, Susan, "Identity Crisis," *Albuquerque Journal*, June 24, 2000, p. B-1.

Chapter Six
Computer and Internet Fraud

The proliferation of computers has led to a new crime: computer theft. Your computer might be stolen during a burglary, along with personal or proprietary information it contains. If you have a laptop, it might also be stolen from your home or business, or taken from you while you're traveling. All it takes is a moment's inattention while you're on a subway, train, or even in a restaurant, for a thief to lift it quietly and vanish.

A common scam today is stealing your laptop while you're moving through the security checkpoint at an airport. You place your carry-on luggage, including your laptop, on the conveyor belt of the X-ray machine, empty your pockets, and move

Computers are a hot theft item, but the personal information contained within your computer can be even hotter yet. There is a recovery system that plants a special program in your computer to identify it, and trace it if a thief uses it to log on to the Internet.

An information thief doesn't have to steal your computer to make off with its intellectual property. All he needs is a few minutes alone with it.

The Internet has spawned a variety of new frauds made possible by the nature of the net. Serious frauds include credit card fraud, hacking, and viruses to sabotage a company's computer.

Hackers specialize in defeating security systems to gain access to targeted computers.

through the metal detector. As you're doing this, the laptop arrives at the other end of the conveyor belt, and a thief lifts it while you're not looking.

The loss of your computer is bad enough, but it's a limited loss. You're out the cost of replacement, if it's not insured, but the information contained within your computer can be very important and lead to losses beyond the value of the machine. If you use the computer to store personal financial records, including your bank account numbers, credit cards numbers, Social Security number, and other vital information, the thief can use this to charge purchases to your credit card accounts, or to drain your bank account. If you use the computer for business, and it contains proprietary information such as customer lists, product designs and specifications, or other sensitive information, you stand to lose far more. Proprietary information can end up in the hands of a competitor, and this can cost your business a lot.

In 1999, over 300,000 laptops were stolen, as well as about 44,000 desktops. The cost of computer theft is high, estimated at over $1 billion a year, with intellectual property valued at another $15 billion. According to the FBI, about 97 percent of stolen laptops are lost forever.[1]

There is a recovery system that plants a special program in your computer to identify it. This program is not detectable and resists tampering, even if a thief suspects that the program is embedded in the computer. The program takes less than 64 KB on your hard drive, which makes it unobtrusive. If the thief uses the computer to log on to the Internet, the computer sends a signal to the Computer Trace Monitoring Center in Canada, including the telephone number from which the signal originates. This tracing takes place even if the thief breaks up the computer for parts, as the program is on the hard drive, and if the drive is used on another computer, it will still send out the recovery signal if connected to the Internet. The CompuTrace Program has a recovery rate of over 90 percent.[2]

The program is available from:

> Absolute Software
> 13920 SE Eastgate Way, Suite 110
> Bellevue, WA 98005-4400
> Phone: (800) 220-0733

Information Theft

A corporate spy doesn't have to physically steal your computer to make off with the information it contains. A corporate spy posing as a temporary employee can rifle your electronic files if he gains access to your computer. A device resembling a portable CD player is actually a CD writer that can record the contents of your hard drive if the spy can connect it to your computer's parallel port for a few minutes while you're at lunch. As an additional ruse, the CD can contain music on the first band, in case anyone becomes suspicious.[3]

The Internet

The Internet has spawned an entirely new category of con games, made possible by the characteristics of the Internet. One relatively harmless one is web site advertising. Ever notice that when you log on to many web sites, the advertising banners download instantly, but the material you're seeking takes much longer, leaving you staring at the screen for many seconds or even minutes? Think this is merely because the system is slow?

It's intentional, because Internet advertisers know that once they have you hooked, they can keep you staring at the monitor waiting for your material to download. They also know that a certain proportion of people will respond to their ads.

On some sites, the plethora of advertising banners is so pro-fuse that they're called "banner farms."

More serious frauds include credit card frauds, "hacking," and viruses to disrupt a company's operations by sabotaging its computer. The National Consumer's League has estimated that consumers lost over $3.2 million during 1999 to Internet fraud. This came along with a 38 percent increase in Internet fraud complaints that year.

Banks are often targets of computer fraud, because that's where the money is. The House Banking Committee reported that U.S. financial institutions get ripped off via computer theft at a rate of $2 billion a year. One reason for their vulner-ability is that they don't have the right kind of software to ward off fraudulent transactions.

Hackers

"Hackers" are computer experts, sometimes self-taught, who crack security systems to gain access to others' com-puters and retrieve information from them. Hackers have tech-niques for obtaining passwords to defeat the computer's secu-rity, and even develop methods to gain access through "back doors," vulnerable areas in computers. Hackers have been re-ceiving a lot of attention lately, partly because they're very dangerous, and partly because they appear glamorous. After all, the high school student who defeats the security of a De-fense Department computer seems like a juvenile Robin Hood, and there has been at least one Hollywood film produced on this theme. This film was *Wargames*, with Matthew Broderick and Dabney Coleman. The plot was that a bored, under-achieving high school student hacked into his school's com-puter to raise his grades, and progressed to gaining access to the main computer at North American Defense Command, inadvertently starting a sequence of events that almost launched World War III.

Hackers are significant threats because of several factors. One is the proliferation of hardware, as today many people have computers wired into the Internet, adding to the pool of potential victims and hackers alike. The computer with a modem is the doorway into hacking, and some exploit them for this purpose. Another factor is that the hacker community is well organized, with exchanges of information on breaching computer security.

There are several schools for hackers located in remote places such as Manila, Pakistan, and Serbia. Serb hacker sites attacked NATO computers during the recent Kosovo fracas, saturating them with floods of e-mails that disrupted them. Mainland Chinese hackers spread viruses into Taiwanese computers very recently.[4]

Another reason is that countermeasures against new threats take time to implement, and viruses spread within hours. Hackers can cause much damage before computer security experts devise ways to defeat the latest attack.

Hackers fit into several categories. One is the recreational hacker, who does it for fun. Another and more dangerous type is the institutional hacker, who is the cutting edge of organized crime or a competitor's employee who specializes in damaging computers or stealing information from them.

There are two types of threats from hackers. One is the "unstructured threat," by "script kiddies," who play with computers and obtain gratification from overcoming security systems. These operate networks over which they boast of their successes and compare techniques for defeating security systems. They can cause a lot of damage, but are not truly sinister in purpose.

"Structured threats" are more serious because they come from several sinister parties. Organized crime can blackmail corporations, threatening to disrupt their computer operations unless they pay. Industrial espionage is another structured threat. A company may seek to steal a rival's client list, engineering designs, and other sensitive information for its own benefit. Terrorists may attempt disruption to advance a political agenda, sabotaging a utility company's computers to cause interruptions of service, or damaging a government's computers as a form of protest. Structured threats are the more dangerous because they're better organized than high-schoolers just having fun.

Among the structured threats are national security threats, conducted by hostile intelligence agencies, "information warriors," and those bent on creating a "Computer Pearl Harbor." A hostile intelligence service may seek entry into a government computer to obtain sensitive information or to install a virus that can be activated to damage it in case of war. Rumor has it that Coalition hackers did exactly that to Iraq's air defense computers during the Gulf War. Military use of viruses is top-secret, so no hard information is available. For example, a recent article in *Time* magazine by General Wesley Clark (American Commander in Kosovo), laid out futuristic combat techniques including stealth aircraft and smart bombs, but made absolutely no mention of computer warfare.[5]

An article in a professional publication quoted John Serbian, Jr., a CIA information operations issue manager, as saying that countries such as China and Russia are developing Internet warfare capabilities. Countries militarily weaker than the United States would try to level the playing field by disabling command centers and sabotaging information systems, thereby partly neutralizing American military effectiveness. However, Serbian did not say anything about U.S. information warfare abilities.

Hackers use many techniques. One rudimentary technique is "dumpster diving," rummaging through a target's garbage in the hope of finding documents with passwords and other information that can ease illicit entry. Another is the "brute force" method, a computer program that can try many likely passwords in rapid sequence to effect entry. There are "sniffer programs" that eavesdrop on a target's telephone lines to pick up addresses and passwords. Another technique is called "social engineering." A hacker will telephone a company's computer system operator claiming to be an employee who has forgotten his password. Psychological manipulations of various sorts also fall into this category.[6]

Once into the target's computer, the hacker can try to take control, erasing data or issuing spurious commands to disrupt operations. He can also use a program to download data from the target computer, a technique very useful to an industrial spy. If he's skilled, he can purloin data without the victim's being aware of it. However, many of today's sophisticated computer security programs maintain activity logs that will alert the owner to unauthorized activity.

Detecting and investigating computer security breaches requires a specialist. The computer detective will scrutinize system logs to see who has been gaining access, and to recognize unusual patterns of use. He'll be careful not to turn off a hacked computer, because it may still have the hacker's program running in its Random Access Memory (RAM). He'll also scrutinize carefully any messages recently received, to trace their sources and to see if they contain any Trojan horses.

The revenge hacker doesn't fit into any neat category. One recent instance was a man sentenced to probation after setting up a spurious World Wide Web page in his ex-girlfriend's name that included pornographic pictures that had been doctored to show her face. He also had set up an e-mail account in her name and solicited sex in her name by responding to online personal ads.[7]

Computer hacking is a growth industry, and recent events bear this out. Various viruses have disrupted operations of several Internet services, and caused interruptions of service. They have attacked private individuals, sending out spurious e-mails with malicious program codes that disrupted the computers of those who received them, then replicated themselves to go out and disrupt other computers.

Not all computer theft and information stealing is the fault of hackers. A major problem is stealing by "insiders," dishonest employees. Some instances are minor and even funny, except for the fact that they add up to a lot of money. Today, employers worry about personnel logging on to porno sites during working hours, thereby stealing their time.

A survey of companies revealed that the number of unauthorized uses of computers by insiders and outsiders was about the same, from 1996 to 2000.[8] These included financial fraud, sabotage, information theft, denial of service, and unauthorized access.[9]

A confusing factor is the number of undetected losses. Because of their situations, insiders have a better chance of carrying out an attack and of getting away with it than outsiders. If the insider is a computer systems specialist or security director, the chances of getting away with it are very good.

Malicious Code

When logging on to some web sites, you may see a dialog box on your screen warning you that the download may contain a "malicious code," and asking if you wish to continue. A malicious code can be anything, from a virus to a sequence of instructions that disable a function on your computer. One example is a code from a web site that disables your "Back" button, trapping you in that web site. This is just an advertiser's trick to make it harder for you to ignore the ads. Dealing with this isn't very hard, though. First, you bring up your "History" file, then double-click on a previous page. This will usually get you out of that web site. Next, of course, you remember that web site and don't go to it again.

This is a simple example of a "Trojan horse," a sequence of signals sent to you to serve the web site's purpose. Some Trojan horses do more than trap you in the web site, however. One kind remains in your computer, periodically sending back information from your computer, such as the sites you've visited recently. This is called an "E.T. Program," because it calls home.[10]

Usually, you're not aware that your privacy has been invaded, simply because you cannot scan everything that you download. The E.T. program can slip in, unseen, and the only clue you'll have is if your modem light flashes when you're not doing anything. That alerts you to the fact that something is going out, somewhere, but you need sophisticated computer tools to find out exactly what's happening.

E.T. programs are used by marketers who want to know your computer browsing habits, anything you buy online, and other information the program can cull from your computer. Of course, marketers like to pretend that this activity is harmless, and that they don't keep data on individuals, but if you believe that, you might be a potential buyer for the Brooklyn Bridge. Actually, once a marketer collects information on you, he can arrange it as he wishes, compile lists of people who visit certain web sites, and other lists of those who buy certain products online. These he can sell to whom he wishes.

Again, what harm does this do? That depends on you. If you visit certain porn web sites, do you want this information to end up in a database, available to anyone who wants to buy a list? Anyone can buy a list, even police. Next time a sex crime takes place in your area, you may be on a list of suspects. How about certain politically sensitive web sites, such as one operated by the Ku Klux Klan or a militia? You may be poking around out of casual curiosity, but the result may be surprising. The person or organization operating the E.T. program may be compiling a list of political extremists.

Let's also note here that you do not have to visit a web site that anyone would label "pornographic" or "extremist" to end up on somebody's list. If you visit a web site that contains information about AIDS, do you want to end up on a list of suspected homosexuals? If you visit a web site with information about Viagra, do you want your name on a list? What about depression? If you look up information about depression online, your privacy is not as assured as if you looked up this information in a public library, or bought a book on depression in a bookstore.

Keep in mind that employers today are constantly searching for new ways to gather personal information about applicants. Often, they use a "shotgun" approach, indiscriminately gathering data that may have nothing to do with an applicant's qualifications or work record. Urine tests are a good example, because they were instituted on the pretext of detecting illegal drug users but have other uses.

Ostensibly used to weed out users of illegal drugs, urine samples can provide much information about the applicant's health. However, there is sometimes a hidden agenda. Urine can be tested for diabetes, for example, as well as other medical conditions. An employer concerned about the number of sick days an applicant might take, or the cost of company-paid medical insurance, may well want to know this. Some tests are even more invasive. Testing a hair sample can reveal illegal drug use as long as nine months ago, long before an applicant presented himself or herself for the job.[11]

Urine tests are not the only hazard. Computer databases allow intrusions into your privacy without your even being aware of them. Today, there are many private security firms employed to check out applicants for employment. Their reports include such basic information as criminal records, credit reports, and verification of home addresses. However, with the many databases available online, it's easy for such a firm to conduct a computer search and find out other things about the applicant. The explosion of online databases has shattered the traditional concepts of privacy.

For example, check out the commonly available online telephone directories. You'll see ads for services that offer other information as well. These include previous addresses, lists of neighbors with their addresses and telephone numbers, court records, etc. These online checks are available for $30 or $40 per name. There are also other services, catering to private investigators, that offer much more information. A look in the Yellow Pages will disclose a listing of private investigators specializing in computerized checks.

E-Mail Pitfalls

E-mail is today a standard communication medium, faster than the post office's "snail mail," and lending itself to various abuses. Some employees have sent sexually harassing e-mail, or arranged to sell their companies' proprietary information via e-mail. This is why employers today often scrutinize their employees' e-mail. This is important to you because you cannot rely on the privacy of your e-mail at work. If you're an employee, don't write anything in your e-mail that you wouldn't want to see published in your newspaper, because it's almost certain that someone, somewhere, is reading it. Even if your company does not monitor its e-mail, you're not out of danger. It can happen at the other end. If you send a personal e-mail to a friend at another company, his employer's security officer may be reading it.

While the courts have established that an employee has no expectation of privacy while using the employer's computer or e-mail system, not every company monitors employees' e-mail. The latest *Security Management* survey showed that 73.7 percent of companies have policies regarding employees' use of e-mail. However, only 28.4 percent said they monitor employee use of e-mail, and only 16.3 percent actually read employees' e-mail.[12]

Even if you do not use e-mail at work, you're vulnerable to e-mail viruses because the viruses are indiscriminate. Recent years have seen the appearance of several viruses that have attacked the systems of corporate, institutional, and private recipients. The notorious "Melissa Virus" was one.

The basic security technique against an e-mail virus is to delete the message without opening it. However, hackers have devised methods of defeating this. The trend in e-mail viruses is to search the computer's e-mail address list and to send a virus-infected message to all on the list. This is especially dangerous because the recipient sees an e-mail from someone he knows, and this disarms suspicion.

The "I Love You Virus" used exactly this technique. It replicated itself and sent e-mail to everyone in the victim's address book. Another virus was the "Janet Simons Virus," recognizable by the subject line: "Resume- Janet Simons." According to the FBI's National Infrastructure Protection Center, the virus deletes some of the victim's files, then sends a copy of itself to everyone in the victim's address book.[13]

Viruses are not frauds, strictly speaking, because many of those who generate viruses do not do so to earn money. However, an organized crime group could menace a corporation or a university's computers, threatening to take down their computers unless the victim paid a ransom.

There are also various kinds of fraudulent e-mail, again not necessarily sent to earn money, but for various personal motives. We'll examine these later.

Spam Tricks

"Spam" is an unsolicited advertisement received via e-mail, the electronic equivalent of junk mail. On the surface, this may appear harmless, because you can always delete unwanted messages. However, when your incoming basket is cluttered with spam, it becomes a major nuisance to delete all the traffic. Unfortunately, spamming is legal. Right now, there are no laws against electronic junk mail. The only restrictions on spamming are conditions of use laid down by various Internet Service Providers (ISP) such as Flashnet, America Online, and others, who do not want their computers cluttered with millions of unpaid advertisements. They'll cut off the service of any subscriber who sends mass e-mailings without their authorization.

Some ISPs have "warning flags" to alert them to any subscriber who sends much more than the average number of e-mail, while others have limits on the number of people to which an e-mail message may be addressed. They will actually block transmission if you try to send an e-mail to more than, say, 20 or 40 addresses. Their purpose is not to protect you, the consumer, but themselves. ISPs sell advertising space to businesses, and they don't want their facilities used for a purpose for which they do not collect money. Spammers piggy-back on an ISP's e-mail system, depriving them of potential revenue.

The main reason spam exists is because it's the cheapest form of advertising available. Spammers charge a few hundred dollars to reach literally millions of people, and this is much cheaper than sending junk mail through the U.S. Postal Service, or hiring people, even at minimum wage, to make junk telephone calls.

With ISPs hostile to spammers, why do they still exist? One important reason is that they use electronic trickery to disguise the origins of their spam, making it much harder for ISPs to track them down and sue them. They use fake addresses, or work through another party's computer to avoid revealing themselves. Another is that spam works. As long as some people respond to spam advertisements, spammers will thrive. From this, it's easy to see that if nobody bought anything advertised via spam, these concerns would go out of business very quickly.

Spammers use several little tricks to generate mailing lists. One is a program to pick up the e-mail addresses of all those who post messages on computer bulletin boards and "chat rooms." This is why many who browse such sites are very circumspect, "lurking" to read other's messages but not posting any of their own.

Another way of generating a mailing list is to use a computer program that sends spam to all possible combinations of letters and numbers. Most will not reach anyone, but the perpetrators of this scam use a little trick to determine which addresses are active. Included in the message is a line that says:

"If you do not want to receive further advertisements, reply to xxxxxx@xxx.com to have your name taken off our list."

This is a lie. The purpose of this instruction is merely to get you to confirm that yours is an active e-mail address, and you will go on a premium list of confirmed addresses that will be sold to other spammers.

What can you do to help protect yourself from having your e-mail inbox flooded with spam? Actually, there are several common-sense security measures you can take to make life harder for spammers. One is to buy an anti-spam program for your computer. These are electronic filters that delete messages that look like spam to them. The program scans each incoming e-mail for catch phrases such as "Make money fast" and "Incredibly low price."

Some programs are adaptable. You can program them to filter out messages that come from addresses that have previously sent you spam. Some e-mail services, such as "Hotmail" and "Yahoo," have a command to block any future messages from the return address of any messages you select.

Some anti-spam programs produce unwanted results: They block legitimate e-mail. In some ways, this is a worse problem than receiving spam, because important messages you want to receive get lost in your system. If you're running a business, this can hurt you. All told, you can't put much faith in these programs.

Countermeasures often merely give rise to counter-countermeasures. Spamming is a technique of electronic warfare akin to mail-bombing, and for every action, there is a reaction. Spammers have learned to spoof spam detection programs using several techniques. One is to misspell key words in their catch-phrases, such as "Incredibly low price." This will allow it to get through the spam filter. Another technique is to always send a new batch of spam from a different and often spurious address. This tactic defeats the programs that block messages from a list of addresses previously used for spam.

Another way to help defeat spam is to learn about your Internet Service Provider's anti-spam policy. Many have an e-mail address to report abuses, and exhort their subscribers to forward any sales messages to them for action. Flashnet, for example, instructs subscribers to forward the message, with the complete header (the paragraph showing the message's origin and routing) to NO-SPAM@flash.net. The ISP's technicians then will try to track down the spammer.

There are several steps you can take as an individual to defeat spam. The first, of course, is never to respond to spam in any way on the Internet. If you buy something, you're supporting the spammer. As we've seen, if you respond to the instruction regarding having your address deleted from the mailing list, you're playing right into the spammer's hands.

However, let's say that there's no such instruction. Let's also say you're really angry and impulsively want to give the spammer a piece of your mind by replying to the e-mail address he lists in his message. Chances are that you'll receive that e-mail back within minutes as "undeliverable." Right, Sherlock! It was a forged e-mail address, which shows you how devious and unscrupulous spammers really are!

In any event, it does absolutely no good to complain to spammers. That's about as effective as cursing out a telemarketer who telephones you at dinnertime to sell you his product. These people really and truly don't care how irritated you are, and insults roll off their backs. You're just wasting your time cursing them out, unless you use a method that costs them money or consumes their time.

Also, do not "flame" the Internet Service Provider listed as the spammer's point of origin. As we've seen, it's likely that the spammer has forged the address anyway, and you'd just be insulting innocent people.

If you join a "newsgroup" or chat room, never leave your correct e-mail address with your message. Spammers have programs that scan posted messages for e-mail addresses, from which they compile their mailing lists. Sophisticated newsgroup users will list their e-mail addresses as: tomjonesnospam@aol.com or something similar. In their messages, they'll instruct anyone who wants to contact them to delete the "nospam" from their e-mail address. This is something that has to be done manually, thereby defeating any automated collection programs.

Yet another way is to set up a special e-mail address to use only for posting to newsgroups. That way, your personal e-mail address will not be exposed to spammers, and if that special mailbox also becomes cluttered with spam you can simply stop using it.

If the spammer provides an 800-number for replying to his ad, by all means reply, but not from your home phone. The reason is that your telephone number will appear on his next phone bill, and will go on a list of people to call. Instead, call the 800-number from a pay phone and chew him out as profanely as you wish. He'll have to take your call and pay for it too, which will run up his operating expenses without providing him with a listing he can use. This tactic will make his business less profitable.

If the spammer provides an address for sending him orders and checks, obtain a change of address card from your local post office and fill it out, giving a fictitious address in another city. This will re-route his incoming mail, wrecking his business. This is like the technique recommended in various revenge books, but is much safer for you personally because there is no direct and traceable link between your target and you. A suspect list would consist of all the millions of people to which he had sent his spam.

Fraudulent Internet Credit Card Purchases

Anyone who wants to charge to your credit card account no longer has to steal your credit card. All he needs is your name, account number, and expiration date to place orders for merchandise over the Internet. Police tend to be both slow and reluctant to investigate this sort of crime because the investigation can become very complex and time-consuming. Indeed, one expert in the field advises police investigators to assess "whether the effort invested is worth it given the complexity of tackling these types of investigations."[14]

Some law enforcement agencies, such as the U.S. Secret Service, have the expertise but often will not accept cases amounting to less than $100,000. In any case, the Secret Service sees the bank as the victim, not the consumer, because in theory the bank reimburses the consumer for the loss.[15]

Making the tracking down of Internet criminals more time-consuming and difficult is that there are ways of gaining access anonymously to the Net, using various services called "anonymizers" and various other kinds of electronic trickery.[16]

Identity Theft

You'd be surprised what someone can find out about you using the Internet. There are services available to list not only your name and address, but also your credit card numbers, real estate you own, arrest and conviction records, medical records, and other data about you. Private investigators and employers are not the only ones who make use of these databases. Using your identifying data, a fraud artist can run up charges in your name, as well as steal directly from any accounts you own.

As with many other types of serious crime, identity theft is underreported in the media, and when it is, it's often misrepresented, especially in fiction. The movie *Day of the Jackal* depicted identity theft by a professional assassin who needed several passports to cross national frontiers. More recently, *Arlington Road* showed a terrorist who stole the identity of his deceased friend to cover up a criminal past. While assassins and other criminals do steal or "borrow" identities to mask their true identities and elude pursuit, the overwhelming bulk of identity theft is for profit.

The problem is growing. In 1995, there were 8,806 arrests for identity theft, and in 1997 the number had grown to 9,455. Financial losses increased from $442 million in 1995 to $745 million in 1997.[17]

Identity theft is a growing threat in several ways. It lends itself to organized crime applications. It's more difficult to track because it often ties in with other types of scams such as credit card and check frauds. The growing threat from identity theft seems to be directly linked to technology, specifically the Internet, and this also means that it has become a multinational crime. Perpetrators in one country can steal the identities of people in another, and use them for criminal purposes.[18]

The identity thief begins by finding out about you. He may track you through the Internet by gaining access to databases containing your name, address, Social Security number, and bank account numbers. However, this isn't the only method available to the identity theft artist. He can find out what he needs by digging through your trash. He can pick your pocket to obtain your credit cards. He can watch you punch in a telephone credit card number. He can also use pretext calls to obtain information about you over the telephone, either by scamming you (see "Credit Card Frauds") or from a merchant.

Some identity theft rings place a member of the gang in a low paying but critical position with a credit reporting bureau. This provides opportunities to purloin the names, Social Security numbers, and other data about potential victims.

Another type of identity theft was the vehicle for an insurance fraud ring. State Farm had to sue to recover up to $350,000 from 36 people who had participated in an insurance scam. The scam artists stole a New York man's identity to obtain insurance policies, then staged crashes in order to file claims on the policies. As many as 45 people were involved in the "crashes," and these led to 11 lawsuits against State Farm for alleged pain and suffering.[19]

Previously, identity theft was limited because it was very hard to pass another person's credit card to a merchant who knew him by sight. It was necessary for the fraud artist to physically travel from one location to another to make multiple purchases. The fraud artist had to show his face and sign a sales receipt. The merchant may also have asked for supporting documentation, such as a driver's license. The advent of telephone and Internet shopping has changed this radically. Today it's possible to make legitimate or fraudulent purchases sight unseen.[20]

Italian police arrested an Italian couple in Catania, Italy, in connection with identity theft and Internet fraud. This involved credit card numbers of Americans used to place hundreds of thousands of dollars' worth of bets with an online betting site in Bergamo. The couple had winnings of almost $400,000, all at someone else's expense. Hackers had obtained the credit card numbers from Chase Manhattan Bank and Citibank Universal Bank.[21]

Identity theft is a versatile technique used by criminals to perpetrate many types of fraud. These include worker's compensation fraud, insurance fraud, election fraud, food stamp fraud, investor's fraud, student loan fraud, cellular fraud, check fraud, and many others. All evidence shows that the problem is growing, not diminishing.

Hoaxes, Time Wasters, and Predators

The anonymity of the Internet has helped spawn a nasty kind of deviant who enjoys putting over hoaxes, individually or en masse. Without fear of reprisal, the hoaxer can send misleading messages (mental hot-foots, so to speak) that waste people's time or cause needless anxiety. Frauds don't have to be moneymakers.

The Internet has provided a happy hunting ground for predators, people who seek to defraud on a personal level. Con artists who used to employ newspaper personal ads now haunt Internet chat rooms and meeting places.

A computer bulletin board provides opportunities to meet other people online, and to exchange views and personal information. It also allows scammers to prey on victims from behind a shield of anonymity, because there's no way of checking out any statements made by someone online. Many in chat rooms operate using "handles," obvious assumed names, and one fraud artist can "work" the same chat room under several aliases. This allows the scammer to pursue several relationships at the same time, without any of his victims being aware that he's playing a double or triple game.

These deviants do not carry out their schemes solely for monetary gain, but often for the satisfaction of having fooled one or many persons, depending on the nature of the scheme. At the individual level, the hoaxer places ads in various "singles" web sites, trolling for lonely people to answer. These can be "singles" clubs, as well as various sites catering to the sexual fringe. When a fish bites, the hoaxer leads him or her on, reeling in his victim before breaking off contact. In extreme cases, the hoaxer may even make an appointment to meet his victim, then not appear. There is a subculture of phonies who enjoy teasing their victims, setting up relationships, which they exploit to cause their victims pain or anxiety.

In sexual chat rooms, the opportunities for hoaxers and scammers are endless. Some troll for victims by leading them on and asking that their contacts send them sexually explicit photographs addressed to a mail drop. Once the hoaxer receives the pictures, the victim never hears from him again. The hoaxer can send any photographs received to other contacts, passing them off as his own. It's highly unlikely that the victim can prosecute such a scammer. Asking for such photographs is not illegal, and the victim is not likely to want to complain to the police, anyway.

Some predators are very sinister, preying on children. Child molesters have found that the Internet provides access to children, some of whom are vulnerable to "grooming." This is a process of identifying potential victims and softening them up by gaining their confidence. The predator feigns interest in the child, his interests, and even his problems, eventually leading to a personal meeting where he molests the child. Child molesters have been networking through computers for at least two decades, operating out of sight of most law enforcement officers.

Some hoaxers are police officers, posing as minors and patrolling the chat rooms to troll for child molesters. They'll pretend to play the molester's game, warming up to him and agreeing if the predator asks to meet them. When the molester appears at the agreed meeting place, he'll find himself arrested.

Some hoaxes are for-profit enterprises run by criminals. They seek to lure their victim to a place to mug him or her. Another method is to coax the victim into sending the hoaxer money. The criminal may state that he very much wants to meet the victim, but doesn't have the money for travel. The victim sends a check or money order to an address, which is probably a post office box or a mail drop, and never hears from the contact again. This is why many bulletin boards, chat rooms, and various online clubs post warnings at the top of their sites. They advise people to be extremely careful when replying to anyone they meet online, and stress that they cannot verify any information about those who post messages. Some warnings state outright never to send any money to anyone met through the site. Luckily, this type of hoax doesn't find many victims because most people realize intuitively that all they know about an Internet pen pal is what he wishes to disclose. This imposes an attitude of caution.

Other for-profit hoaxers work for legitimate companies to ferret out proprietary information. One technique long used by industrial spies is the "phantom interview" in which an industrial spy poses as a recruiter. Luring employees of rival companies with the promise of a job opening, the fake recruiter asks them probing questions about their current work under the pretext of exploring their qualifications. The "job offer," of course, is totally bogus, but the credulous employee eager for a better job may be reluctant to risk his prospects by asking firmly for the recruiter's bona fides.[22]

The current version of this scam takes place on the Internet. There are commercial job referral services, as well as job listings put out by various trade and professional associations, such as the American Society for Industrial Security. Fake recruiters place ads and wait for responses. When someone bites, the fake recruiter may e-mail him a questionnaire, or even arrange a face-to-face interview during which he "pumps" the job-seeker about his employer's proprietary information. Although this practice is highly unethical, there's no law against it. This is another example of how organized crime blends in imperceptibly with legitimate business.

In 1995, the FBI set up a sting operation to identify industrial spies seeking access to trade secrets. FBI Special Agent John Hartmann posed as a "technology information broker" and received an approach from a Taiwanese company seeking to penetrate the trade secrets of an American pharmaceutical company. The Taiwanese company sent a series of e-mail to Hartmann to obtain the desired information. During a face-to-face meeting with the Taiwanese representative, Hartman informed him that it would be very expensive to license the technology he was seeking. The Taiwanese let slip that he would seek other ways to obtain the desired information. Then Hartmann told the Taiwanese that he had found an employee of the American firm who would provide the information for $20,000 and a royalty on future sales. Hartmann arranged a meeting with the Taiwanese representative and another FBI Agent posing as the corrupt employee. When they met, the bogus crooked employee produced some documents marked "confidential" to offer the Taiwanese. At this point, FBI Agents arrested the Taiwanese.[23]

All of this goes to show that you don't really know with whom you are dealing on the Internet. The Internet's anonymity allows a male to pose as a female, an adult to pose as a child, and a company spy to pose as an executive recruiter.

At times, the industrial spy may even offer a rival's key employee a real job, to elicit the information he holds. This is cost-effective only if the patsy has truly valuable information to provide.

On a group level, the hoaxer originates or forwards chain letters, "virus warnings," and urban legends to cause undue concern to recipients. There have been several spurious viruses named in hoax warnings. One is the "Deeyenda Virus," and the warning claims that the FCC has issued an alert, and that any recipient should delete a message with "Deeyenda" in the subject line without opening it. The message continues to state that anyone who downloads and opens a "Deeyenda" message will have his hard drive obliterated.

There are also urban legends posted on the Internet. Some are stories in newsgroups or online chats. Others seem to be chain letters, with instructions to "Forward this to everyone you know."

Some of the cruelest hoaxes are medical. Today, many people search the web to discover information that applies to an illness they have. Some of the information, placed by reputable medical associations, hospitals, or foundations, has a solid scientific basis. However, anyone can set up a web site offering cures for any disease.[24] Practicing medicine without a license is still illegal, but the difficulty in prosecuting, or even finding, a medical hoax artist is often insurmountable, especially if the hoaxer resides in another country.

Cryonic preservation is a good example. There is a medical theory that a human being can be deep-frozen and revived at some time in the future. The first part is scientific fact. It is possible to deep-freeze a human body. The second part, reviving the frozen body, is purely speculative. Nobody's done it yet, as only sperm and eggs have survived freezing so far. However, the promise is that science will some day discover a way to bring a frozen human being back to life. Some advertise on the Internet. This appeals to someone with an incurable disease, who may want to submit to a deep freeze in the hope that he'll be revived in the 25th Century and cured. Deep-freezing can appeal only to those with the money to pay for it, as the individual must pay the cost of freezing and the cost of maintaining the frozen body at proper temperature for many years, most likely centuries. Some have been able to pay for this cold storage up front. Others have signed over their life insurance policies or other assets.[25]

This is why it's important to check out any item you receive that fits any of these descriptions. Contact one or more of the sites listed in the "Resources" chapter to verify whether or not an online warning or story you receive is a hoax.

Notes:

1. Harmon, Alan, "Restricting Computer Theft," *Law and Order*, May 2000, p. 43.
2. *Ibid.*, p. 43.
3. Holstein, William J., "Corporate Spy Wars," *Online U.S. News*, February 23, 1998.

4. Cohen, Adam, "School For Hackers," *Time*, May 22, 2000, pp. 59-60.
5. Clark, Wesley, "How Will We Fight?" *Time*, May 22, 2000, pp. 98-99.
6. Bottom, Noel R., CPP, "The Human Face of Information Loss," *Security Management*, vol. 44, number 6, June 2000, p. 52.
7. "Man Sentenced For Porn Home Page," *Albuquerque Journal*, June 3, 2000, p. E-3.
8. Power, Richard, *Computer Security Issues & Trends, 2000 CSI/FBI Survey*, Computer Security Institute, 2000, p. 4.
9. *Ibid.*, Page 5.
10. Cohen, Adam, "The Spies Among Us," *Time Digital Supplement*, July 2000, p. 34.
11. The corporate security director who discussed hair testing with the author is an incorrigible snoop, a borderline crank who seeks out any information he can about his company's employees and job applicants.
12. Neeley, Dequendre, "Tech Talk, Polling Corporate Practices," *Security Management*, vol. 44, number 6, June 2000, p. 39.
13. Associated Press, "E-Mail Systems Infected By 'Janet Simons' Virus," Saturday, May 27, 2000, *Albuquerque Journal*, p. A-12.
14. Pettinari, Cmdr. Dave, "The Basics of Investigating Credit Card Fraud on the Internet," *Police & Security News*, May/June 2000, p. 62.
15. *Ibid.*, p. 64.
16. *Ibid.*, p. 63.
17. U.S. General Accounting Office Report, *Identity Fraud: Information on Prevalence, Cost, and Internet Impact is Limited*, May 1998, (GAO/GCD -98- 100BR).
18. National Fraud Center, *Identity Theft: Authentication as a Solution*, p. 2.

19. Newsedge Corporation, "State Farm Sues 36 in Connection With Auto Fraud," March 11, 2000.
20. National Fraud Center, *Identity Theft: Authentication as a Solution*, p. 3.
21. *Ibid.*, p. 5.
22. Holstein, William J., "Corporate Spy Wars," *Online U. S. News*, February 23, 1998.
23. *Ibid.*
24. Engel, Peter H., *SCAM!*, New York, St. Martin's Press, 1996, pp. 109-110.
25. *Ibid.*, pp. 115-116.

Chapter Seven
Stockbrokers

Stockbrokers enjoy good reputations, and indeed many are honest people, licensed to operate their trade. However, you have to be cautious when dealing with a stockbroker, not only because a few are crooks, but because many are subject to various pressures and temptations that put you on the losing end. Also, as we'll see, some "investment advisors" and "investment counselors" are not stockbrokers, but con men.

The stockbroker is supposed to be your agent in stock and bond trades, and your financial advisor if he's a "full-service" stockbroker. "Discount" brokers offer minimal services, not including financial advice. A discount bro-

Most brokers are honest, but you do need to be aware that there are a few out there waiting to take your money.

Do your homework, but beware of the following:

- Speculative stocks
- Mutual funds
- Get rich quick schemes
- Aggressive annuities
- Account "churning"
- Online investing or day trading
- "Limit Order"
- Mail-order advice on stocks and the stock market
- Investment advisors and counselors
- Pump and Dump

ker is legitimate, but offers less service than a full-service broker. You get what you pay for.

Your stockbroker may suggest that you invest in certain stocks, according to your investment aims. If you're looking for safe, low-risk stocks, he may suggest investing in various big-name companies or conservative mutual funds. On the other hand, if you're looking for quick money, he may suggest investing in "speculative" stocks and mutual funds, which offer the prospect of greater returns but also greater risks. In plain language, you may get rich quick, but you may also lose your shirt.

Your stockbroker is not independent, because he works for a brokerage firm. He has to take orders, as does any employee, and his manager may be "pushing" a particular stock or fund that week. The firm may have been hired as an agent to sell a certain company's stock, or mutual fund. It also may be the agent for an issue of municipal bonds. This in itself isn't illegal or even unethical, but be careful if your stockbroker tries to "push" you into investing in any sort of securities you don't know.

One example is the stockbroker who recommends that you invest in a mutual fund operated by his own firm. His manager may have ordered him to "push" that fund this week, to build up business. Getting new people to invest in that fund will drive up its price, to the benefit of the company.

Another example is an aggressive annuities fund. Your stockbroker may telephone you and tell you that taking your money out of one annuity and putting it into another will get you a cash bonus. This may be to your advantage, because you receive cash in hand for making the switch. At this point, the question to ask yourself is whether the stockbroker is also getting a premium for bringing in customers. You may choose to ask him directly, but be prepared for an evasive answer.

Protecting yourself against stockbroker scams is basically passive. Beware of any effort to "push" you into investing in an unfamiliar fund or stock, especially if your stockbroker telephones you out of the blue to recommend it. Learn what you can about the stock or fund, such as how long it's been in business and how it has fared in the market.

On the other hand, if you ask your stockbroker for recommendations, you're on slightly safer ground. There's still no guarantee that he'll make an honest recommendation, and you still have to be careful, but at least you know he's not running a full-bore selling effort against you.

Keep in mind that these stockbroker tactics are not illegal. Stockbrokers are well represented in the Securities and Exchange Commission (SEC), the federal agency that regulates them. They make the rules, and the rules they make allow them a lot of latitude.

One outright fraud is "churning" your account. Stockbrokers operate on commissions, and what they sell is what they eat. Obviously, the more transactions they make, the more they earn. Commissions are a percentage of every transaction, and the important point to keep in mind is that brokers collect their commissions up front when you make the transaction. The stock's subsequent performance is irrelevant, because their commission is linked to the value of the stock when you trade, not to any money you may earn or lose.

The flagrantly dishonest stockbroker will try to push you into as many trades as he can, because that's how he earns his money. If the stock goes down the toilet and you lose your shirt, too bad. This is why you must avoid letting yourself be pushed into many transactions. If the stock is worth buying, it's usually worth holding, because you'll be earning dividends on it. Over the long run, you'll also be earning as the stock appreciates in value. This is called "capital gains" and is taxed at a lower rate than earned income. On the other hand, if you're buying and selling every week, the risks are far greater and the only person earning sure money is the person who collects the commissions.

Some investors now use the Internet. They get online with their stockbroker and order purchases and sales of stocks and bonds. Some "day traders" innocently believe that their orders will be executed as soon as they hit the "Enter" key, but that's not so. As Arthur Leavitt, Chairman of the Securities and Exchange Commission, recently pointed out in a series of "Investors Town Meetings" held in various American cities, there are pitfalls. If a day trader enters an order to buy a stock he sees offered at a favorable price, by the time the order is executed, the price may have risen. In today's volatile market, this is very likely, and the investor will find that he's bought it at a higher price than he'd been led to expect. Likewise for "sell" orders. By the time the broker actually sells the block of stock, the price may have dropped to where the profit margin is gone. The only protective measure he can take, according to Leavitt, is to enter a "limit order," specifying the price at which the stock will be purchased or sold.

Another activity that is legal, although dishonest, is the touting of stocks and systems for making money in the stock market. A stock tout will write books on how to make millions in the market, and some of the more brazen ones even hold seminars and sell tape cassettes (at a healthy price) telling you how you too can earn millions by wise investing. A moment's reflection should tell you why you should view their claims with suspicion, and not send them money to obtain their advice.[1]

Why would anyone who has a sure-fire system for getting rich in the stock market bother to share his "secrets" with you? Why would he want to waste his time trying to teach others his system when he'd be better off practicing his system to become rich himself? The answer, of course, is that he can earn more money selling his system to others than in using it himself, which tells you something about the validity of stock investment "systems."

Investment Advisors

There are legitimate investment advisors and counselors, but be aware of a crucial difference. They are not necessarily licensed stockbrokers. The title is often used by stockbrokers working for legitimate companies, and by legitimate advisors working independently, but also by some scammers.

Henry was a fraud artist, purely and simply. He was a fast talker who operated by word of mouth, taking advantage of affluent acquaintances. His mode of operation was to persuade an affluent victim that he would be able to "invest" his money for him and bring him returns well above average. Instead, he simply took the money and used it to buy himself a house and live an affluent life. Because Henry was a criminal psychopath, his sense of reality was deficient, and he didn't realize that he could not keep up his game indefinitely. The clever fraud artist takes the money and runs, but Henry remained in the area, living the high life, until one of his victims complained to the district attorney's fraud unit. A criminal prosecution resulted in Henry's having to give up the assets he'd stolen and spending eighteen months in the state prison.

When he was paroled, he took a job as an advertising salesman for a weekly newspaper on the brink of bankruptcy. In his new position, he hinted that he'd be able to help the owner financially by drawing upon a million dollars allegedly in a Swiss bank account. He used this promise to keep his job, as he was a notoriously unproductive salesman, and he made many overseas telephone calls, chatting with friends in foreign countries, before the owner tired of the game and got rid of him.

One way to tell if an advisor is legitimate is to determine how he earns his money. If he charges you an hourly rate for his advice, he's probably legitimate. If, on the other hand, he earns his money from commissions on your investments, he has a definite interest in pushing you to make as many transactions as possible, and may not be legitimate. If he refuses to disclose this information to you, he's almost certainly a scammer.

Pump and Dump

This is a stock inflation scheme that has been with us a long time, but the Internet has given it new life because it's now possible for one scam artist to run it by himself. The classic pump and dump technique is for a dishonest brokerage company to buy up the stock of a worthless company traded on the stock exchange. The next step is to have the company merge with another, also worthless, but with a product that could be hyped to make it appear as if the company was about to take off big-time. One current category that has investors panting is bioengineering, for example. Using this as a selling point, the dishonest brokerage company sells shares at inflated prices to gullible investors. The rush to buy would feed on itself, with more investors swarming to buy shares before the price peaked. Once all the shares were sold, the price would find its own level, as there would be no more investor push to drive its price up, and usually the price would drop catastrophically.

Running such a scam used to require a large sales force, and lots of money. Today, the Internet has made it easy and cheap for the scam artist. Two California men pleaded guilty to securities fraud after being caught at this game. They bought a bankrupt Dallas printing company, NEI Webworld, for 13 cents a share, then placed messages on Internet bulletin boards hyping the stock. Gullible investors responded by buying the stock, driving the price to $15 per share. The two perpetrators of this scheme were able to sell the shares they held for a profit of $364,000. The same day, the price of the stock fell to 25 cents per share.[2]

It's a sure bet that others will repeat this scheme. With proper precautions to make identifying them difficult, future scammers will exploit the peculiarities of the Internet to generate illicit profits.

Notes:

1. Engel, Peter H., *SCAM!*, New York, St. Martin's Press, 1996, pp. 119-120.
2. Brown, Jeff, "Net Makes A Stock Scam Just A One Person Job," *Albuquerque Journal*, July 27, 2000, p. 20.

Chapter Eight
Unbundling

"Unbundling" has evolved into a soft-core scam that usually is perfectly legal, but basically dishonest. It's hard to say who began the practice, but today the prime suspects are attorneys and hospitals. Let's look at attorneys first.

One attorney joke has a 33-year-old lawyer at the pearly gates, protesting that he's too young to die. Saint Peter asks his age, then remarks:

"Funny, but according to your billing records, you must be at least 85-years-old."

This illustrates the practice of "unbundling," sometimes called "incremental billing."[1] A text-book case showing how this

"Unbundling," sometimes called "incremental billing," is usually legal, but is basically dishonest. Attorneys and hospitals are best known for this practice.

A lawyer who works for a "bargain" rate may add charges for various nickel-and-dime items, such as postage or photocopying. With these "incidentals" added to the bill, he's no longer a bargain.

Hospitals are notorious for this practice. In addition to charging you for a daily room rate, they will bill you for absolutely everything they do for you, including drugs and other supplies. One hospital billed a patient $10.50 for a pint of hydrogen peroxide, the same brand selling for 85 cents in the hospital's lobby pharmacy.

works took place ten years ago during a divorce action. The husband's lawyer charged $160 per hour, while the wife had found a bargain basement attorney who charged her "only" $135. However, to her dismay, the wife found that her lawyer was also billing her for court filing fees, every photocopy he supplied, postage, and a number of other nickel-and-dime items. The bottom line was that the wife's lawyer cost her about as much as the husband had paid for his.

The wife's lawyer was within the law, although what he did was dishonest. Attorneys know the law, and know exactly what they can get away with, unlike many other scam artists. They know that their clients are mainly interested in their hourly rates, and usually fail to ask about "incidental" expenses, so the lawyers simply don't tell them. They also don't tell them the fine points about their billing practices. Lawyers bill by the hour, and in fractional increments. If you telephone your lawyer to clarify a point, or even just to ask when your court appearance is scheduled, you'll find that he or she has charged you for the time spent on the phone call. If he writes a letter on your behalf, or just reads a letter you've sent him, he'll bill you for that. These nickels and dimes add up faster than you're likely to anticipate, which is why lawyers often ask that you pay them a "retainer," several thousand dollars against anticipated fees and expenses.

Hospitals are also notorious for this practice. Upon entering the hospital, you'll probably know what the daily room rate is. However, what they don't tell you is that they'll bill you for absolutely everything they do for you, including drugs and other supplies. One hospital, for example, billed a patient $10.50 for a pint bottle of hydrogen peroxide, the same brand selling for 85 cents in the hospital's lobby pharmacy. The net result is that you may be anticipating a bill for $500 a day for your hospital stay, but when you get your final bill, you'll find that the cost is several times that.

Unbundling is a scheme with a future. It's not illegal, and takes advantage of the fact that many people will accept a simple answer, without inquiring into ramifications that can cost them much more than they'd expected.

Notes:

1. Engel, Peter H., *SCAM!*, New York, St. Martin's Press, 1996, p. 12.

Chapter Nine
Retail Store Scams

False advertising is illegal. With that established, we also have to note that retailers get away with it literally every day of the week. How many times have you trekked to a retail store in pursuit of an advertised "special," only to be told that they were "sold out"? How many retailers have been prosecuted for this? Have you heard of any?

A basic principle of retailing is to get the customer into the store on whatever pretext is possible, because retailers know that once inside, a certain percentage of customers will "impulse-buy." That's why the come-ons and other tricks.

Apart from illegal acts, retailers have other tricks to get you to buy more. Supermarkets place everyday staples such as milk and meat at the back of the store

You get a stack of ads in your daily newspaper and decide that you are going shopping!
Buyer Beware!

This chapter points out the various scams you should be watching for:

- Advertised "specials" that are gone in a short time
- False advertising
- Hard-to-find specials put way in the back of the store
- Impulse buying
- Aggressive merchandizing, constantly moving the merchandise
- Pricing "errors" with the UPC

to force you to walk down the aisles, knowing that something is likely to catch your eye and you'll buy it on impulse. Another way is to place displays to obstruct the aisles, forcing you to slow down and look at them. Yet another way is to make advertised specials hard to find, placing them in out of the way aisles, forcing you to walk up and down several aisles before you find them. They know that the more time you spend in the store, the more you're likely to impulse-buy.

Still another technique of aggressive merchandising is to re-arrange the items every few weeks. Retailers know that many shoppers who work with shopping lists become familiar with the store layout and go directly to the items they need and ignore the rest. Store managers frustrate this by moving the items around, thereby defeating the efficient shopper and keeping him in the store longer.

Pricing "errors" have been facilitated by the introduction of the Universal Product Code (UPC) during the 1970s. Bar codes, as they're known colloquially, make it much easier for the cashier to ring up sales. Instead of reading each price off the item, the clerk passes it over a scanner, which reads the item and assigns a price to it. One benefit to the retailer is that he can hire lower-grade help, because the computer performs all the calculations, even figuring out the amount of change to give the customer.

The dark side is that when you shop this way, the items go by in almost a blur as the clerk passes them over the scanner. Even if you remember the prices on all of the items you buy, you hardly have time to check if the price displayed is the correct one. If you really want to know if you've been charged the correct prices, go over each item when you leave the checkout aisle, comparing them for errors.

The "errors" can come about two ways. First, the manager enters the wrong price into the central computer. The other way is by not entering the sale price when an item goes on special, instead charging customers the full price. If you complain to the manager, he'll shrug and mumble "computer error."

When you find an error, chances are it will be in the store's favor. Retailers know that many customers are too harried and preoccupied to check their cash register receipts, and this lets them get away with over-charging. Try this yourself. Whenever you see a discrepancy between the advertised or displayed price and the register slip, note whether it's in favor of the store, or in your favor. Most people who have done this have noted that in almost every case it's in the store's favor.

"Let the buyer beware" is still true. Don't believe for a moment that a large retail firm is above scamming you. Keep your eyes open, even when you make routine purchases at your local supermarket. Above all, read ads skeptically!

Chapter Ten
Media Scams

Anyone who believes that our media are dedicated to bringing the American people the "truth" is naïve. Media insiders talk about "info-tainment," reflecting that even supposedly serious news programs and documentaries exist to entertain as much as to inform. The corollary is that the bottom line is all-important, and if you can make a buck by selling junk, it's better than going broke telling the truth.

An outstanding example is the sensationalizing of news. All experts in the field agree that violent crime has been dropping during the 1990s, yet the news programs emphasize violent crime, because this is what sells.

For the media, making big bucks is more important than telling the truth. This is why the media sensationalizes the news, emphasizing violent crime, even when violent-crime rates are dropping.

Beyond the straight news media are the bottom feeders, dealing in stories so sensational as to be absurd.

Controversial or sensational events or personalities may result in a spate of articles or books making outlandish claims.

Usually such literary trash is worth reading only for amusement. However, if you believe every claim for miracle health cures, you may get yourself into trouble if you don't investigate further.

Videotape of red lights flashing and corpses being brought out on gurneys grips viewers, and as the purpose of the news media is to capture audiences for advertisers, "body bag journalism" is on the rise.

Apart from the straight news media, there are the bottom feeders, dealing in stories so sensational as to be absurd. One example is the array of articles that appeared after the end of World War II claiming that Adolf Hitler had not really perished in Berlin, but was alive and well in Argentina, Paraguay, or other countries. This earned some writers many bucks but the theme has dwindled in recent years because if Hitler were by some miracle alive today, he'd be over 110 years old. However, that hasn't stopped the Elvis sightings. We still see an occasional article claiming that Elvis Presley is still alive somehow and living in an obscure location.

Any controversial or sensational personality or event is likely to result in a spate of articles, or even books, containing outlandish claims designed to attract the attention of credulous people who will then buy the publication. The John F. Kennedy assassination, for example, resulted in hundreds of books and thousands of articles, many with bizarre theories regarding the motives, methods, and outcome of the killing. Some even claimed that President Kennedy was not dead, but merely brain-damaged by the bullet and surviving on a Greek island. These fabrications sold tabloids.

During the 1960s, there were magazines devoted to the real and imagined activities of Kennedy's widow. People labored in offices dubbed "Jackie Factories" to pound out articles speculating on whether or not the widow was happy, who she was dating, and whether she was likely to remarry, etc. "Jackie" stories were always worth a headline, true or not, and they sold papers.

Most of the time, this sort of literary garbage is worth scrutinizing only for amusement. If you're reasonably intelligent and level-headed, you know that sensational articles about celebrities and their sexual scandals are literary junk food. You can read them for laughs while standing in a checkout line, then put them back when you reach the cashier. These concocted stories are not always that harmless, though.

These literary scam artists can hurt you when it comes to reporting on health matters. If you read about a new herbal cure for cancer, or a fad diet, and take it seriously, you can become very sick before you realize that the article had no scientific validity. This is why you have to be skeptical regarding what you read.

Chapter Eleven
The Nigerians

There is one recent fraud that takes direct aim at people who are avaricious and believe that they can get something for nothing. These people lack the judgment to screen out obviously phony offers.

During recent years, a barrage of scam letters has come out of Nigeria, directed at affluent Americans. The typical letter reads like this, paraphrased to correct grammatical errors:

"Dear Mr. XXXXX;

This letter is to seek your help and to offer you an opportunity to earn some money by acting as my agent in a financial transaction. The Government Purchasing Commission had authorized me to procure some heavy equipment for Nigeria's economic development and furnished me with funds to do so. After making these purchases, I found that I had ten million dollars left

Many Americans have received letters from Nigeria.

- There are variations on the scam, such as sending you a letter stating that a "problem" has developed which can be solved if you send money to the writer.

- In some high-tech variations, you may receive the letter via your fax or e-mail.

- Never reveal your banking information to a stranger.

- Never respond to such letters.

- Be wary of all "something for nothing" offers.

- Contact the postal authorities or the U.S. Secret Service, if you receive such a letter over. I'd like to transfer these funds into your account so that I may recover them later. In return for your help in this matter, I will pay you a 10 percent commission. To let me transfer these funds electronically, please send me your bank account numbers, as well as the banker's name, telephone, and fax numbers."[1]

This is a scam, pure and simple. Once you send the numbers, the scam artist will use "bank drafts" to "vacuum clean" your accounts. This technique is now getting old, and your banker should be wary of sending any customer's money overseas in response to a bank draft.

This has led to other variants on the scam, such as reeling you in once you've shown interest. You'll receive a letter advising you that a "problem" has developed, and which can be solved by sending money to the writer. The "problem" may be a government official who has to be bribed or an unforeseen tax that has to be paid. If you send money to the scam artist, you'll never see it again. The chances of your recovering the stolen money are non-existent, because by the time you discover that you've been had, the money is in Nigeria, completely out of your reach.

There are now high-tech variants on this scheme, according to the Better Business Bureau. You may receive a letter from another country, such as New Zealand or Brazil, and the appeal may be sent to your fax machine. You might even get it via e-mail. This is why you have to be wary of all "something for nothing" offers.

The only protection you have against such a fraud is to be very suspicious when offered easy money. Never reveal your bank account numbers to anyone you don't know, whatever the reason, and be especially careful with appeals such as the Nigerian fraud. Above all, never travel to Nigeria in response to such an appeal, as Nigerian gangsters have been known to extort money from Americans under threat of violence.

What do you do if you receive such an appeal? First, do not reply, under any circumstances. It's simply too good to be true. You may then send the letter to your local Postal Inspectors. The U.S. Secret Service would also like to hear from anyone who has received Nigerian scam letters or faxes. You may forward it to:

U.S. Secret Service
Financial Crimes Division
1800 G Street NW
Washington, DC 20223
Phone: (202) 435-5490

What good will this do? Frankly, it will do very little. The authorities already know of this scheme, as the Secret Service receives hundreds of phone calls and pieces of mail about this each day. The U.S. Government cannot prosecute outside the United States, and will not even make the effort, unless the crime is some sort of high profile atrocity on the scale of the Pan American airliner bombing over Lockerbie, Scotland. It will also respond to an attack on a high U.S. Government official, or the bombing of an embassy. As far as protecting the little guy, the hard fact is that you are your first line of defense.

Notes:

1. Taken from a letter recently received from Nigeria by the author.

Chapter Twelve
Advertising and Marketing Frauds

Advertising is merely the art of creative lying, as has been documented many times in prosecutions against fraudulent advertisers. However, because advertising is "legal" organized crime, advertisers are always several steps ahead of the law. Advertising by its very nature is deceptive, and many advertisers perpetrate frauds against you that are perfectly legal, although not legitimate. An example is the junk mail designed to look like a check. This often comes in a brown window envelope, and the document inside looks like a check, to make you open it. When you do, you find that it's a "voucher" for magazine subscriptions or the like.

> Advertising is the art of creative lying. Many advertisers perpetrate frauds that are legal, but not legitimate.
> Below are some of the various scams out there to entice you:
>
> ■ Junk mail designed to look like it contains a check.
>
> ■ Answering surveys and filling out registration cards only adds you to someone's mail list somewhere.
>
> ■ On the Internet, the advertising banners always download first and you're a captive audience.
>
> ■ Each web site you visit deposits a "cookie" in a special file in your computer.

Let's remember that the main task of radio, TV, and the movies is to capture audiences for advertisers. Their purpose is to grab your attention, and entice you to read or watch advertisements. A magazine story will begin near the front to "hook" you, then lead you off into the back pages where one column of text laces between several columns of advertisements. At times, even the "news" media use absurd stories to attract audiences because they know that there are many stupid and credulous people out there for the plucking. A recent example that will become a classic is the "Y2K" hoax, during which many mainstream media ran stories predicting awful disasters that would come with the new century.

We also see this tactic used on the Internet. You log on to a web site, and the advertising banners always download first. You're a captive audience, and the advertiser believes that you'll sit there reading his ads while waiting for the rest of the information to appear on your screen. Often he's right.

Compiling Marketing Lists

The stock in trade of many merchandisers today is mailing lists. Merchandisers, especially those engaged in direct mail, know that the key to profit is not to waste valuable printing and postage on unlikely prospects. They want to confine their mailings to tightly focused lists of potential customers. A simple example is the merchandiser of baby items, who understands that any advertisements sent to people who don't have small children are utterly wasted.

Merchandisers use various techniques to gather information, and most of their information comes from you. They know that they can trick people into providing information about themselves that they normally would not disclose. One trick is the registration card supplied with appliances and other products. These often contain long questionnaires, asking how many similar products you own, how many there are in your family, your buying habits, and your total household income.

Merchandisers count on many people not knowing that they don't have to provide such information to make the guarantee effective.

Another trick is the "free drawing," offering a high-dollar item as the prize. To be eligible to win the car, or home entertainment system, all you have to do is fill out an entry form. The form asks many probing personal questions, such as size of your family, income, etc. For the merchandiser, this information is valuable because it contains up-to-date names and addresses, and he can sell the lists he compiles for many times the value of the "prize" he gives to the winner.[1]

Another tactic, legal but insidious, is the "shopper's card" offered by many supermarket chains. Merchandisers are so eager for you to sign up that they'll often offer you a bonus, such as a two liter bottle of soda pop, to fill out their forms and receive your discount card. With this card, you'll get a few cents off the prices of various items, hardly worth the trouble of filling out the form. However, it's definitely worth the trouble to the supermarket chain, because of the information these cards provide.

Every time you go through the checkout line, the clerk scans your card with the bar code reader, and then scans all of your purchases. This provides the supermarket with an up-to-date picture of what you're buying. This information is priceless to merchandisers. A sudden flurry of baby food and diaper purchases, for example, strongly suggests that you have a new baby in your home. It may not bother you that the supermarket is compiling lists of new parents, but keep in mind all of the other items that supermarkets carry that provide clues to your lifestyle. Do you want them to track your alcohol purchases? Do you want them to know how often you buy condoms? Do you want every prescription you have filled at the supermarket pharmacy to go into a merchandiser's database?

Other tactics edge closer to outright fraud. One is the "free" long-distance calling service offered by several Internet suppliers. They claim that you will be able to make long-distance calls all over the country by signing on to their service and buying a headset that plugs into your computer. When you gain access to the site, you find that you have to fill out a comprehensive questionnaire that asks for a variety of personal information, including your name, address, age, members of your family, household income, etc., before being allowed access to the service. They also ask you what magazines you read, whether you invest in the stock market, and what hobbies you pursue. When you finish answering the questions, you find that the service doesn't work as claimed.

However, it works for marketers. They now have detailed information about you, which enables them to provide advertisers with tightly focused mailing lists according to your situation, needs, and interests. Special interest mailing lists are among the most valuable properties for advertisers, and they'll go to great lengths to compile them. Manufacturers of baby products, for example, seek lists of people with infants, because they're more likely prospects than lists taken from telephone directories. Makers of golf equipment will pay for lists of golfers.

If you use the Internet, you may not know that each web site you visit deposits a "cookie" in a special file in your computer. These cookies tell Internet merchandisers a lot about your interests and your needs. Your cookies are open to inspection by any web site you visit, and the merchandisers are there to build up profiles of people who browse the net.

Notes:

1. Engel, Peter H., *SCAM!*, New York, St. Martin's Press, 1996, pp. 58-59.

Chapter Thirteen
Fund Raising Organizations

The old phony charity scams have been with us forever, but there have evolved some new twists. A plethora of charitable organizations exists today, ostensibly to help various classes of needy people, but their main function is to assure an affluent lifestyle for their staffs. Likewise, various social, professional, and activist organizations have sprung up, and their main activities revolve around fund raising.

Some organizations raise tens or even hundreds of millions of dollars per year, and it's not surprising that their top executives have six-figure salaries. More, they spend money on creature comforts, such as a new headquarters building and millions of dollars of furniture for it.

Many charitable organizations' main purpose is to assure an affluent lifestyle for their staffs. According to an Associated Press survey, the median salary for the top executives of these nonprofit groups was $207,990 in 1999. This isn't illegal, but some supporters might not approve of how their donations are spent, if they knew.

If you support such a group, you should keep informed about the functions and finances. One way is to send for the organization's annual report, which should reveal its income and expenditures for the previous year.

If you receive frequent fund raising letters from an organization, the best defense is to drop them in the round file.

According to an Associated Press survey, the median salary for the top executives of these nonprofit organizations was $207,990 in 1999. This means that half earned more, and half earned less. Salaries ranged from $1,731,922 on down. Benefit packages and expense accounts were in the tens of thousands of dollars. These organizations included charities, hospitals, universities, community service organizations, and others.

It's important to stress that there is nothing illegal about this. People who run charitable, political, and social organizations simply have a good thing going, although some members might not approve of the way their money's being spent, if they knew.

If you're a member of such an organization, it's important to keep yourself informed about its functions and finances. It's especially important to do so if the organization keeps sending you fund-raising letters. One step is to send for a copy of the organization's annual report. This should disclose how much money the organization took in the previous year and it should list its expenditures.

What do you look for in such a report? The first is the salaries of the top executives. If they're getting six-figure salaries, are they really worth the money? Also look at the names of other top staffers. Do they seem to be related to the CEO? If so, maybe the real purpose of the organization is to provide incomes for the family. Another item to scrutinize is travel expenses for its officers or board of directors. Do they travel tourist class, as do the rest of us peons, or do they always travel first class, as if they were royalty?

Another category is expenses with vague descriptions or explanations. If you see that the former Director or President is being paid "consulting fees," there's reason to wonder exactly what "consulting" this person has performed. Is a "consulting fee" merely a sort of pension payment, or free income for a family member?

At times this information will be hard to obtain. You may have to rely upon secondary sources, such as the news media, to provide a glimpse at the high lifestyles of the top organizational personnel. If, for example, the media report the organization's annual convention and mention that the top executives stayed at the most expensive and lavish hotel in the city, you can ask yourself what these pampered directors and officers do to justify the expense.

What can you do if you receive a succession of fund-raising letters from an organization to which you belong? The best defense is to drop these letters into the round file. Don't tell yourself that you'll write a check just this once, to appease them. That doesn't work because fund-raising letters are computer-generated, and the computer is programmed to send letters to those who respond. The net result is that, if you're a frequent contributor, you go on a special "sucker list" and you'll receive appeals much more frequently than if you ignore them. The more you give, the more they want.

Some charities are total frauds. Their directors choose names to resemble that of a real charity, and collect money from well-meaning, trusting people. None of it goes for the charitable purpose.

One "charity" mailed leaflets asking people to "sponsor" a child in a third world country. For $20 per month, they could support a needy child, providing food, clothes, and even schoolbooks. In return, the contributor would receive one letter per month from the child, to express his appreciation. Alternatively, the benefactor would receive a monthly report on the child's progress.

Although many sent their money to support needy third world children, the program was totally bogus. Some aspects seemed incredible from the start. It's hard to believe that an uneducated third world child in an undeveloped country would immediately begin to write letters of appreciation in English to his benefactor.

Chapter Fourteen
Miscellaneous Scams

Fraud artists are constantly coming up with new ways to separate people from their money. At times, these schemes are so convoluted that it's hard to see through them. One is the "fake accident" scam, actually a variation on an old theme that seems to have taken hold in California.

You're driving along on the freeway in your luxury car when a car ahead of you gradually slows and comes closer to your front bumper. When it suddenly slams on its brakes, you run right into it, as the purpose of its slowing down had been to cut your reaction time and make the collision harder to avoid. You pull over, and provide the driver with your driver's li-

Fraud artists keep coming up with new ways to separate people from their money. One is the "fake accident," in which the driver of the car in front of you maneuvers you into hitting him from behind when he sets his brakes. Several people are in his car, complaining of neck injuries, and later you and your insurance company are hit with a huge lawsuit.

Tourists are often targets of scammers. In Lake Louise, a tourist town in Alberta, Canada, fraud artists posing as plainclothes police demanded to see tourists' passports, credit cards, and money, which they "confiscated" under official pretext.

cense number, address, and insurance information. You notice that there are several people in the other car, all complaining of neck injuries.

Days or weeks later, you find yourself and your insurance company slapped with a huge lawsuit, for damage to the other vehicle, but mainly for whiplash injuries to its occupants. You may not realize that this was a set-up, with a fake insurance claim ring looking for obviously affluent victims. They're in collusion with a dishonest medical doctor or chiropractor to file claims of injuries and expensive treatment required for the "victims." Some of these rings will even hire entire families of immigrants to be their "victims," because they know that their job opportunities are limited and some will take the opportunity to earn a few hundred dollars for a few hours' work.

One of today's common scams has been made possible by the security practices at airports, which came into being only about three decades ago. Passengers going through the metal detectors often have to stop because they have metal in their pockets, suit buttons, etc. While they're preoccupied emptying their pockets or submitting to a search with a hand-held metal detector, they're not watching the items they had laid on the conveyor belt leading through the X-ray machine. While many carry-on items have little value, some are very valuable, because people take cameras and laptop computers on board with them. The alert scammer, hanging around at the fringe of the crowd, quickly spots the traveler whose attention has been diverted by security personnel, and snatches the valuable item off the end of the belt.

Travelers are especially vulnerable to scams because they're unfamiliar with the laws and customs in the places they visit. In particular, they don't know what police I.D. looks like, and they're often unfamiliar with currency and traffic laws. Criminals eagerly take advantage of this, sometimes by posing as police officers.

Lake Louise, a tourist town located in Alberta, Canada, recently experienced a series of police imposter scams carried out by predators who victimized tourists. Posing as plainclothes police officers, they demanded to see tourists' passports, credit cards, and money. Under official pretext, they "confiscated" the passports and other valuables. The passports went into the underground fake document industry, while the credit cards and cash allowed the fraud artists to make purchases at their victim's expense. The Royal Canadian Mounted Police Detachment at Lake Louise responded with a "media blitz," advising tourists that any police officer approaching them in Lake Louise would be in uniform, and by setting up decoy operations to trap the scammers.

At times, the scammer is a real police officer. Foreign tourists traveling the "Arizona Strip," a section of Interstate 15 cutting the northwest corner of the state, sometimes found themselves being stopped by an Arizona Highway Patrolman several years ago. He would politely inform them that they had committed a traffic offense, and would write them a citation. This officer, knowing that in some countries police collect the fines directly from the motorist and that the ticket is merely a receipt, would take their money and send them on their way. At the end of the week, he turned in his tickets to the Fredonia, Arizona, Justice Court, calculating that the tourists would be out of reach.

This officer had not counted on the persistence of a clerk of the court, who sent letters to the offenders in their countries, requesting that they pay their fines. Some of the tourists replied, saying that they had, indeed, paid their fines to the nice officer, and the picture became clear. The officer was immediately fired. However, he was never prosecuted because of the difficulty of getting the victims back from their far-off countries to testify against him.

We're all familiar with the window envelope containing a document designed to look like a check, to entice us to open the envelope and read what's inside. The "check" turns out to be a voucher for a magazine subscription, and is worth absolutely nothing. Now, there's a new wrinkle on the check scam.

You open the envelope and find that the document really is a check, totally negotiable, and made out to you for five or ten dollars. But wait! Before you sign it, carefully read the fine print. You'll discover that by endorsing the check, you're subscribing to a service. It may be a long-distance telephone service, or you may be signing up for a credit card with a sky-high interest rate, or something else you neither want nor need.

Again, this points up the need to be skeptical when faced with an offer that appears too good to be true. Always look for the hook.

Chapter Fifteen
Protecting Yourself

Self-protection begins with an attitude of carefully cultivated paranoia. Better believe that "they" are out to get you, because they really are.

The first step is to practice tight security with all personal documents, including your bank statements and especially your checkbook. Never leave your checkbook where a dishonest person may gain access to it. In some cases, this means practicing tight security even at home.

Chuck lived in a house with several other people, including the owner from which he rented a room. He didn't know the other renters very well, and one of them turned out to be a "player." This person got hold of Chuck's checkbook one day

Self-protection requires paranoia, because "they" really are out to get you.

You must practice tight security with personal documents. Keep sensitive items in a safe place.

Any paperwork containing personal identification data should be shredded before it's thrown in the trash. The best security is to shred, then burn, all sensitive documents.

Telephones can be beneficial, or instruments of evil. Remember that when you use a portable phone, you have no legal right of privacy.

E-mail can be vulnerable, but every proprietary e-mail service is "password protected," and you have to type in a secret word to gain access.

If you are victimized by a fraud artist, you will have little or no recourse, so you must be on guard. You are your first line of defense.

and carefully removed one check from the bottom of the pad. As he knew how much money Chuck had by reading his checkbook register, he forged Chuck's name to a check that drained his account. By the time Chuck discovered the theft, the player was long gone.[1]

This incident illustrates the importance of keeping checkbooks, credit cards, and other sensitive materials in a safe place. If you can't keep them on your person, make sure they're locked away. Always remember that, if you leave them in your car, they will get stolen along with the vehicle if your car is stolen. At work, you may leave them in a locked drawer of your desk, but they're only as safe as the lock on that drawer. If you forget to lock it when you leave, you may find your documents missing upon your return.

This is also true of checks you write to pay utility and other bills. If you leave them in the mailbox in front of your house, they're wide open to mailbox theft. A mailbox raider can, in a hit and run operation, collect many checks from a row of mailboxes, use chemicals to bleach them, and rewrite them for his own purposes. There's also another danger, despite the new high-security checks issued by some banks that make forgery much more difficult. The fraud artist who steals your checks has your name, bank, and account number in his hands. Using these, he can vacuum clean your account in the same manner as the Nigerian racketeers.

When you mail checks, never leave them in curbside mailboxes, vulnerable to theft. Always drop them into a secure locked mailbox, preferably one belonging to the U.S. Postal Service. Best of all, deposit them in the post office or a mailbox right outside the post office. Many post office mailboxes have warnings advising customers not to deposit mail after the last pick-up, because some bold mailbox raiders have been known to crack even U.S. Postal Service deposit boxes during the hours of darkness.

The 1990s have seen a great increase in the use of paper shredders. Previously, only government agencies and large corporations used shredders. Today, individuals and small business owners recognize that it's smart to destroy many kinds of documents instead of simply throwing them into the garbage. You can buy a personal shredder at Walgreen's for $19.95, and even an inexpensive shredder is worth the money. "Dumpster divers" can retrieve your account numbers from old checks, credit card receipts, and bank statements, and they can use them to drain your assets.

You should make it a firm rule to shred any paperwork that contains personal identifying data. These include old credit cards, old checks, bank and brokerage statements, correspondence from any of these firms, old passports, old driver's licenses, and many other types of paperwork: "When in doubt, don't throw it out."

There are many brands of shredders, and they vary in quality, capacity, and security. The simplest are entry-level shredders for home use. These slice your documents into ¼″ strips, offering a basic level of security. They will make a credit card or driver's license absolutely unusable by anyone else, but a persistent and patient fraud artist can still piece them together to read your account numbers.

Higher security shredders turn your documents into confetti by using "cross-cut" blades to cut the strips into fragments. These fragments are much harder to piece together, and the task will frustrate and discourage most fraud artists. After all, why should a scam artist spend many difficult hours trying to put together your confetti when your neighbor uses a shredder that produces ¼″ strips?

The best security is, of course, to shred, then burn, all sensitive documents. These include credit card applications you receive unsolicited in the mail. These contain sensitive information, and you should always destroy them before discarding them. Likewise for "checks" made out in your name where your endorsement subscribes you to another long-distance carrier. You may not think this is even worth shredding, but a scam artist may sign it over to himself, and you may find yourself trying to get out of an agreement you never signed.

Defense Against Unscrupulous Retailers

We've studied some of the tricks retailers use to impel their customers to buy more. How can you protect yourself and get back at these sleaze-bags? It's not too hard if you put your mind to it. Let's first look at protecting yourself. The first tool you need is a shopping list. Before you go to any store, write a list of what you need. Once inside, stick to it, and never buy anything that isn't on your list.

If you can't find a particular item because the manager has moved it elsewhere, always ask for help. Always ask, to take up the manager's time, instead of spending yours chasing around the store. Be polite, but make the manager or store employee find it for you. This will consume some of his time, and if enough people do this, store managers may get the message that shuffling items around the store isn't necessarily a smart idea, because it increases their workload. In any event, you save your valuable time by asking. Always keep in mind that retailers think their time is very valuable but they don't mind wasting their customers' time by various tricks.

Retaliation can take several forms. One day, when you have a little time to spare during a usual shopping trip, fill your basket with several items you don't need. Passing through other aisles, drop them off at various points. This will consume the time of a store clerk, who will have to restock the items properly.

If one day you're really angry, perhaps because you had a run-in with your employer or an argument with your wife or neighbor, blow off steam by going into the store and snagging a shopping cart. Fill it with a lot of items, preferably perishable items such as frozen foods. Then leave it in an aisle and walk out of the store. Don't worry about CCTV surveillance or store detectives. Store security personnel are worried about people who walk out of the store without paying for what they're taking with them, not people walking around with a cart inside the store or walking out empty-handed.

Detecting Lies

Frauds, whether economic or personal, always involve lies, whether explicit or implicit. Learning to spot deceptive tactics is another basic step in protecting yourself from fraud.

During the 20th Century, many people developed systems, techniques and even machines for detecting lies. Most of these won't be applicable in your situation, because you won't be able to use them. It's not practical to ask a salesman to allow himself to be hooked up to a polygraph, colloquially and inaccurately known as a "lie detector." Also, it's impossible to attach one to a telemarketer whose appeal sounds interesting. In any event, the telescammer is most likely to be reading from a script written by someone else, and possibly unaware of how much of his script is lies. Although there are "voice stress" machines to detect deception by analyzing the changes in frequencies of the human voice, they're unreliable, as are "polygraphs." The best method available to you is "tactical interviewing," which you can do in person or over the telephone. Although the telephone is more restrictive because you can't see the other person, you can still analyze the content of his statements, and judge whether they hold together.

Tactical Interviewing

There is a step-by-step procedure for interviewing, and following it provides a great advantage in separating fact from fancy. Begin by discussing neutral or harmless topics, such as the weather, or traffic conditions. This isn't aimless chatter, as it provides you with a baseline of normal unstressed behavior, as long as you keep it low-key and don't appear to be pushy. Listen very carefully during the interview. You want to observe the other person's behavior while answering neutral and unimportant questions before you begin the significant questions. Let's note here that establishing a baseline won't work with a telemarketer, because he plunges right into his script.

The difference between hearing and listening is like the difference between seeing and observing. This is a supremely important principle of interviewing: listen very carefully to what the other person asks or says. A lot of people don't really listen during a conversation, instead thinking of what they want to say after the other person finishes. Some turn conversations into games, trying to be witty or intellectual. They spend so much time and effort trying to impress the other person with their cleverness and charm that they miss some very obvious clues. It's very important to retain what you hear, because many people provide verbal clues that are useful if you can only remember and analyze them later.

Watch the person's eyes, and listen to the tone of his voice. Become familiar with his speech pattern, and the normal way in which the person expresses himself. The speech pattern is supremely important in a phone conversation because you can't see the other person. In face-to-face interviews, notice gestures, such as swinging the leg or scratching the face, and note if these are more frequent during difficult questions.

Once you're familiar with the normal speech pattern, you can ask a few significant questions and look for changes in speech or behavior. For example, if the other person normally answers a question immediately, but hesitates or looks at the ceiling when you ask about a certain topic, you know you've hit a sore spot. If the person averts his eyes, fidgets, crosses his legs or arms, or leans away from you, this can indicate a problem. More to the point, the person may be thinking about what to tell and what to withhold. However, let's not exaggerate the importance of physical signs. Body language does indicate stress, but doesn't necessarily indicate a lie. The topic might be uncomfortable for the other party, but the answers might be truthful.

As we'd noted earlier, there are basically two types of lies: lies by deliberate misstatement, and lies by omission. Some people fool themselves into believing that they're not really lying if they merely withhold information.

Many people are not willing to commit themselves to an outright lie by misstatement, instead preferring to finesse it, provide an ambiguous reply, or avoid answering the question. There are several verbal cues that tip you off to evasiveness. We see some of these when you ask a closed-ended question that the other person can answer with a simple "yes" or "no." The most obvious is answering a question with a question:

Q: "Have you ever been divorced?"

A: "Have you?" or:

A: "Why do you ask?"

This is as blatant as it gets. This person is being clearly evasive, and this alerts you that you may have serious problems obtaining straight answers.

This can become comical, such as when you ask:

Q: "Why do you always answer a question with a question?"

A: "And why shouldn't I answer a question with a question?"

Another type of evasion is not answering the question directly:

Q: "Have you ever been divorced?"
A: "I wouldn't say that." or:
A: "I can't say."

Well then, if he wouldn't say that, what would he say? A lot of times, an indirect answer such as this demonstrates that there is a lot to hide.

Yet another type of evasion is this one:

Q: "Do you smoke?"
A: "Not really."

There are several other ways in which people evade truthful answers, or evade questions, meanwhile providing verbal cues. One is to say "That's a hard question." Another is to say, "I'm not that sort of person." Yet another is asserting ignorance in a conditional way, such as, "How should I know?"

Of course, a favorite way of evasion, often occurring in court or during Congressional hearings, is, "I don't remember" or "I can't recall." You can't expect to hear many replies such as this during most situations, because what passes for "truth" in a judicial or legislative setting sounds absurd in normal conversation.

An exasperating way of evasion is very obvious because it's so time-consuming. This is talking around the subject and never getting to the point. However, some people do this habitually, simply because they're long-winded, which is why it's crucial to establish a baseline of normal speech before getting to serious topics. In this case, the person who normally provides short and concise answers to questions reveals himself if he begins to tap-dance around a significant question.

Getting to the truth can be time-consuming, and requires patience. One step is to recognize that there are sex differences in patterns of lies. Psychiatrist Charles V. Ford, M.D., points out that men tend to tell outright lies to exaggerate their importance, incomes, and occupations. Women, by contrast, tend to leave out things to conceal facts about their personal histories, including age and body weight.

Ways of getting at the truth during an interview involve asking many related questions, but not necessarily immediately after a doubtful statement. For example, later in the conversation ask a couple of questions about the other person's occupation, and listen for inconsistencies and contradictions. It becomes more difficult to maintain a lie if one has to invent details.

In cases where you suspect a lie by omission, return to this topic later and ask a direct question about it. You can spot lies by omission by noting logical gaps in the other person's story. This often happens when meeting people who respond to romance ads. For example, the person might tell you that he was divorced in 1990, but say nothing about any relationships between then and now. You can, later in the conversation, ask, "Did you have any relationships between 1990 and now?"

Another example occurs if the man states that his ex-wife withheld sex for years. A gentle way of exploring this topic and finding out if he'd had an affair with another woman is to ask, "How did you cope with this?" and build from his answer. Asking "layered" questions, moving logically from one aspect of the topic to the next, is a good way to elicit information.

Another point to elicit during an interview is mutual acquaintances and friends, or business references. If you find out that the other party knows some of the same people you do, you can check him out with them. Their opinions can be very illuminating, if you evaluate them the right way. Obviously, you can't give as much credence to the opinions of an embittered ex-spouse as you would to someone who hadn't been emotionally involved with the other party. A person dissatisfied with a company's products or services might simply be very hard to please. However, don't overlook derogatory information if it's possible to check out the facts. For example, a former spouse might tell you that the ex had once been convicted of a crime. This is a matter of public record, and you can check it for veracity.

There are other systems of deception detection, as we've seen. One is based upon "kinesics" and other body language and mannerisms. To use this system, you have to be able to see the other person, obviously impossible in the case of a telemarketer. Also, you cannot see the person who sends you an e-mail message or who writes a deceptive advertisement. In any event, these systems are not very reliable either, for a very important reason.

Fraud artists are practiced liars who enjoy deceiving others for both fun and profit. Lying will not induce stress, won't make them become nervous and fidgety, and fraud artists will not display the commonly accepted signs of deception, such as shifty eyes. To detect their lies, you have to use other means, such as fact-checking.

Check the Facts!

There's no substitute for fact-checking. Surprisingly, there are many facts that you can check without much trouble if you know something about the topic or area involved. For example, if the other person claims to have lived in New York City recently, ask how much the subway fare costs. If you've been recently in New York yourself, or know somebody who has, you can check the accuracy of the answer. Another detail open to fact-checking is a mutual acquaintance. If the other party claims to have worked for a company where you know some people, ask whom he knew during his stay there.

Another example is if a stockbroker wants to sell you stock in a company he claims is earning tremendous profits and whose value has been rising, you can check this out by obtaining a copy of its annual report, or getting a profile from one of the on-line financial services. If the company doesn't exist, or if the price of its stock has been declining, you can find this out very quickly and easily.

Always check out claims that are open to fact-checking. Some claims are not. If the claim is that a new fad diet is "tastier than other diets," you can't really check that out because taste is largely a matter of opinion. However, if the claim is that the new diet has been "endorsed by the American Medical Association," you can quickly find out if it's really true. Sometimes, you can ask the salesman to do it for you. Don't hesitate to ask outright: "Where can I see this in writing?" If he fudges, you know something is wrong. That's why it's always a good idea to take the time to check the facts.

To forestall this, the fraud artist will insist that you make a quick decision. He doesn't want to allow you the time to check out his claims. If you find yourself being pressured to "ACT NOW!!!!" it's a 100 percent tip-off that there's something wrong with the deal.

Another technique is to check for inconsistencies. One example that happened to the author was an insurance salesman masquerading as an "investment advisor." He was selling an alleged investment plan and claimed that the investor could withdraw his money at any time with no penalty. However, the brochure stated that there was a 2.5 percent penalty for withdrawal of funds before a specified time limit. The salesman was unable to explain the discrepancy because he'd been caught in an outright lie.

Inconsistencies are always suspect. A woman stated that she was 60-years-old (in late 1996), yet said she was 12-years-old when World War II ended. Simple addition suggested that she was actually 63-years-old in 1996. Both statements could not be correct, and she was obviously shading the truth.

It's also important to understand all the conditions before committing to buy or invest in anything. An ad for a "FREE!!!!" cellular phone always contains fine print that you also have to sign up for a service contract. A rebate on the price of a computer often has a string attached, that you have to subscribe to a certain Internet Service Provider for a specified period. Always look for the hook.

When investing, be especially careful in dealing with investment advisors. Is the advisor a licensed stockbroker? Does the advisor work for a legitimate brokerage firm? Does the advisor have an office where he can be reached? In any case, never hand over money to anyone on the strength of a vague verbal promise. Always get it in writing.

It's very important to be especially vigilant when using the Internet to obtain information about potential investments. As we've noted from the example of the NEI Webworld case discussed in the "Stockbrokers" chapter, dishonest players can use the Internet to pump up the value of a stock. Planting messages praising the stock on bulletin boards and in investors' chat rooms is merely spamming, but it fools some people. Always remember that a posting praising a stock can be merely a manipulative device.

It's worth repeating here that many of the people using chat rooms and bulletin boards do so under handles, not their real names, and that you know nothing about them. While not all people who post anonymously are dishonest, don't invest your money on the word of a stranger.

Another way of detecting a fraudulent claim is judging whether it sounds too good to be true. This is where common sense is crucial. A stockbroker who tries to sell you a stock or bond that will make you incredibly rich would not be wasting his time selling it to you if it were for real. Instead, he would have invested his money and retired for life. A diet that promises quicker weight loss than other diets is unlikely to be legitimate.

It also helps to recognize the basic tactics of fraudulent selling, such as the "come on." A "low introductory interest rate" is merely to get you signed up, for after a specified period the credit card provider will slap you with its normally high rate. "Half-price" offers work the same way. After the introductory period, the cable company or magazine will charge you the normal rate, or even higher.

It's especially important to be vigilant when browsing the Internet. If you're in a chat room, always keep in mind that everything you think you know about a conversational partner is what he chooses to tell you. This is especially true in chat rooms devoted to sex. There are adults posing as children, children posing as adults, men posing as women, and women posing as men. Take nothing for granted.

This is also true when researching a topic, such as cures for cancer or AIDS. The information posted on a bulletin board is only as valid as the person posting it, and the person may describe himself as a medical doctor to appear convincing. However, there's no way to know if the person actually is a doctor. Be especially wary if anyone is selling a "cure" for anything.

Romance Ads

If you're responding to a personal ad in a romance publication or on the Internet, be especially careful regarding scammers. The greatest hazard is not the serial killer or the person seeking to make a financial profit from you, but the person who falsifies information to make himself more attractive. When arranging a first meeting with anyone met through a romance ad, never give your home address. There can be several reasons for this, the most common legitimate one being that if the person is undesirable, you don't want him or her continuing to phone you or coming to your home.

This is where an unlisted number serves a purpose. You may want to feel the other person out before giving him your home address. Another way is for the other to give you his number. However, you may be concerned that he'll "capture" your number with Caller ID. Keep in mind that there's no way to tell if the other party has Caller ID when you place a call.

If you don't want to reveal your number, you have at least two choices, blocked calls and pay phones. The blocked call is one that will not register on Caller ID, either because you have an unlisted number or because you punched in "*67" before making your call. This registers on Caller ID as "Private Call" or "Anonymous Call."

Once your contact provides an address or phone number, you'll want to verify it. The local phone directory is a first step. Another is a city directory, such as Cole's, available in the reference section of the public library. If you have Caller ID, the phone number of anyone who calls you will appear on the display unless it's an unlisted number or a blocked call.

One way of finding out the caller's number even without Caller ID is to tell the caller that you have another call waiting, and ask for a number where you can call him back in a few minutes. This also gives you time to look him up in the phone book or to check with your computerized telephone directory.

If you're arranging contacts by mail, you may wish to use a PO box instead of your home or work address. Women tend to use mail drops and PO boxes more often than men. However, those into exotic sex often use boxes and mail drops to insulate themselves from their correspondents. They don't want someone dressed in leather to show up at the front door carrying whips and chains.

An important point is that you can't find out much about anyone you meet via a romance ad unless you're willing to reveal something of yourself. The more meetings you have, the more you'll exchange information. Remain alert for the person who persistently refuses to give you his home address. He might be hiding something, such as a wife and children.

It's customary for people who contact each other through ads to meet on neutral ground, such as a public place. One good rule is to set the meeting place indoors, at a coffee shop or mall, instead of a park or street corner. That way, you're not waiting in discomfort if the weather is bad and the other party is late or doesn't show at all. To guard against these contingencies, bring a book or magazine with you. Bring your own transportation in case you have to bail out quickly.

A public place also offers some security while you size up the other party. Also, when you arrange to meet someone for the first time, tell a relative or friend where you're going and whom you're meeting. If this isn't possible, leave a note in a conspicuous place at home. These are discreet methods of protecting yourself without offending the other person.

If you're seeking to meet someone for romantic purposes, avoid romance ads and join a club, not necessarily a singles club. Clubs offer other ways to meet people, the sort depending on the type of organization. Obviously, a church group will bring you into contact only with those of your own faith, which can be important if you're very religious. Occupational and professional organizations, such as the American Medical Association and the American Society for Industrial Security, bring you into contact with members of your own occupation. This offers a common meeting ground. However, an organization such as Mensa limits membership to people who score very high on intelligence tests, but often members have little else in common.

Yet other clubs are social, including those specifically for single persons, such as "singles clubs." Some singles clubs are pretty casual, requiring only a membership fee, while others screen applicants and require proof of divorce or death of the spouse to ensure that applicants are truly unattached. The main characteristic of a singles club is that practically everybody you meet, apart from the occasional faker, isn't married.

There is one supreme advantage to checking out potential partners in club meetings. You can observe without committing yourself, noting how your candidate interacts with other people. In a one-to-one meeting, each party is concentrating upon the other one, trying to make a good impression.

It's much easier to observe how a person interacts with others, without being directly involved. When part of a group, it's easy to see the role each person plays. Most groups have a loud-mouth, a compulsive talker who almost never shuts up. You can easily spot undesirables and typical jerks, such as the man who acts as if he's God's gift to women, or the woman who is so impressed with herself that she treats men with disdain and disrespect. The best part about these personality types is that they're so obvious, and you can avoid wasting time with them. There are also other undesirable types, such as confrontational and abrasive people, and it's easier to ignore or to avoid them when part of a group than when you're half of a pair.

You're under no pressure to make a commitment or even ask for a date. This means that you can take your time evaluating possible candidates, and zeroing in on the one who appears best for you. You can spread your efforts over several club meetings without appearing hesitant, indecisive, or anti-social.

Telephone Tactics

The telephone can be a beneficial tool, or an instrument of evil. Today, simply owning a telephone is not enough. You have to use street smarts and have a couple of accessories to ensure your security.

Understanding what a telephone is, and is not, is the first step. Most of your telephone communications will be secure. There are some glaring exceptions.

One is the portable phone, whether it's a radio extension of your house phone or a cell phone. We'll call them "radio-phones" for convenience and simplicity. Realistically, whenever you use a radiophone, expect less privacy than when using a hard-wired phone. Anyone within range can hear you. There may be a neighbor with a portable phone that happens to use the same channel as yours. There also may be a scam artist cruising the streets with a portable, hoping to overhear a sensitive conversation.

You have no reasonable expectation of privacy when you use a radiophone. This has been upheld by court decisions. One Missouri drug dealer found himself arrested during the mid-1980s after a neighbor overheard him arranging drug deals on his portable phone and notified the police. The court held that this was not wiretapping without a warrant because by using the portable phone, he broadcast his conversations over the air, and he was convicted.

This is why you ought always to remain aware of what you're saying when using a radiophone. If you don't want your boss or your neighbor to know about your recent lobotomy or hemorrhoid surgery, don't blab about it on the air.

Another problem is telemarketers. Use your Caller ID to see who is calling you. If you get an "OUT OF AREA" message, chances are overwhelming that it's a telemarketer. Listen while your answering machine takes the call. If it's a legitimate call from someone you know, you can always pick up the phone.

What about striking back at pests who annoy you by calling at inconvenient times? The old trick of asking him to hold because someone is at the door doesn't work any more because it's been so widely used. The salesman will hang up almost immediately when he hears that.

Instead, waste his time by speaking with him. This technique works perfectly if you have a phone in the bathroom because you can waste his time without wasting much of yours. Feign interest in the product or service he's selling, but ask him to repeat himself several times. After several minutes, when you've convinced him that you're seriously interested, tell him to hold for a minute, without explanation. When you return to the phone, ask him: "Still there?" and continue the conversation. Do this several times, asking him to hold while you take out the garbage or do something else useful. Finally, you ask him to hold while you ask your spouse. Come back a minute later and say: "No, my wife won't let me. Sorry," and say goodbye. You'll have wasted several precious minutes of his time by keeping him on a string.

Another problem is the telephone scam artist who tries to obtain bank and credit card numbers from you under a pretext. Never give out any personal information over the phone if you did not initiate the call. Obviously, if you're ordering merchandise by phone from a company you know to be legitimate, it's usually safe to do so. However, if anyone calls you requesting this information, absolutely refuse to give it out. If the caller sounds convincing, and you think he might be legitimate, ask him for a number to call him back. The scam artist will never provide a number. As an extra precaution if the caller does provide a number, check it out in your telephone book to make sure that the number is actually listed to the bank or credit card company.

Computer Security

If you operate a business, you have to protect yourself against hackers who may try to steal your trade secrets by tapping into your computer. Even if you have no trade secrets to protect, the hacker may be after your customer list and their credit card numbers for the purpose of identity theft. The day will come when you can be sued for not taking sufficient care to safeguard customer information.

If you deal over the Internet, you may hire a computer security specialist to install various protective measures such as "firewalls" to keep unauthorized users out of your computer. These security measures are truly not very secure, because with every new security technique, there evolves countermeasures to breach them.

There is only one sure way of keeping hackers out of your sensitive computer files. This is to use one computer to deal over the Internet, and another totally separate computer to store your sensitive information. If there is no direct physical connection between your high-security computer and the telephone lines, there is no way for a hacker to get to it. It's really that simple.

Many companies do not practice tight Internet security because it's inconvenient. They either use a central computer with "workstations" in various parts of their facilities, or store some sensitive information on the computer that is wired into the Internet. Also, using separate computers in a "network" within a facility makes them all vulnerable if one of these connects to the Internet.

At times, it seems impossible to practice tight Internet security. Companies that sell over the Internet may find it very convenient to store customer lists, including their addresses and credit card numbers, on the computer wired into the Internet. This makes the information vulnerable to hacking, as we've seen.

E-mail can be very vulnerable. However, there are some absurdly simple security measures you can practice to make it harder for the hacker to gain access to your e-mail and your sensitive files. Every proprietary e-mail service, such as Hotmail and Yahoo, is "password protected," which means that you have to type in a secret word to gain access. The e-mail function on your computer usually is not, unless you set it up that way.

Many private and business computers also have password security, to prevent a casual user from gaining access to sensitive files. However, some legitimate users make it too easy for the hacker, with stupid mistakes. An example was depicted in the film *Wargames*, in which Matthew Broderick saw the password to his high school's computer written on a slip of paper on the secretary's desk, taped to a pull-out shelf in her desk. Although the password was changed regularly for security, she crossed out the old password and wrote down the new one each time. If you do the same thing, you're leaving yourself wide open to anyone with even momentary access to your office or home.

Another mistake is to throw out any piece of paper with the password on it without destroying it. This leaves you vulnerable to any dumpster diver who rummages through your garbage. If you're a business owner who employs a janitor, he will have easy access to your wastebasket. A standard industrial espionage technique is to employ agents who obtain jobs as janitors to hunt through a competitor's wastebaskets for any important information.

However, even practicing basic security can leave openings that a hacker can exploit. You should choose your password with care, but many do not. They use passwords that a hacker can easily guess. They may use their birthdays, or auto license plate numbers. They may use the initials of their company name, product name, or their street addresses. Some use their wife's or children's names. One electronic company used the password "diode" in its alarm system during the 1960s. All of these are easy to guess intuitively, and a skilled hacker can quickly run through the most likely passwords.

This is why it's important to use a password that a hacker can't possibly know and is unlikely to guess, and which you can easily remember without putting it down on paper where it can be read by a hacker. Some possibilities are the street next to yours but spelled backward, the name of a pet you no longer have, the address where you lived as a child, your favorite food, or your favorite singer.

If you have to use several passwords for access to sensitive files or Internet services, you may not be able to remember them all. In this case, you may write them down, but keep the paper in your safe. A less secure method is to carry the paper in your wallet instead of leaving it where someone might see it. The risk of losing your wallet or having your pocket picked is relatively small, and you may feel the risk is small enough to tolerate. The chances of the person finding or stealing your wallet also being a hacker are small.

Another security technique is to look at the properties of any sensitive file before you open it. Many word processing and other programs record the date and time the file was last opened, and if you see that a certain file was opened during your absence, it's a tip-off that some unauthorized person may have gained access to it.

Computer security also includes protecting your computer and the information it contains from physical theft. While locks and alarm systems can hamper a burglar, and awareness can help prevent theft of your laptop while you're carrying it, you should take additional steps to protect sensitive information because any security system can fail.

No sensitive information should be on your hard drive, because if your computer gets stolen by either an outside thief or an "insider," the information goes with it. All such information should be on a separate disk. For small files, a standard 3.5" floppy will do. However, today's word processing and database programs create such large files that an ordinary floppy disk is too small. There exist "ZIP" disks (high capacity disks) that can hold much larger files. The standard ZIP disk can hold 100 Mb of data, while the high-capacity model holds up to 250 Mb. If your sensitive files are very large, you may choose a CD-ROM drive, using optical disks that can hold up to 650 Mb each.

Keeping sensitive information on removable disks will not work if you leave your disks where they can be stolen with the computer. In the office, all disks containing sensitive information should be stored away from the computer, in a locked drawer or in a safe. Better yet, take them home with you. Disks are small and light enough to carry on your person, in an inside pocket. There are disk wallets available in computer stores for exactly this purpose.

Another problem arises with laptops. Most carrying cases for laptops contain pockets for disks, and if you keep the sensitive disks in one of these pockets, they'll go with the computer. The solution is to use those storage pockets only for blank disks, and to keep the important ones on your person, so that a thief gets away only with your hardware. Another reason for doing this is that airport X-ray machines have magnetic fields that can erase a disk or corrupt the data on it, and you don't want to lose your sensitive files by accident when the security personnel run your laptop through the X-ray machine.

This is why an extra safeguard is to store sensitive information on a CD-ROM. These are optical disks, with the data etched by laser, and they cannot be erased by any magnetic field. A CD-ROM is thinner than a floppy or ZIP disk, although larger in diameter, and is just as easy to carry in a pocket or in your checked luggage.

Internet Security

We've covered some of the scams being used on the Internet. The hard-core scams are outright frauds, while the soft-core scams do not actually ask you for money. Instead, they ask you for personal information that they use to compile marketing lists. One way of making life harder for these people is to fake your personal information.

If you sign on to a "free" service and are obliged to fill in a long questionnaire before being allowed to receive the service, always fake it. If you provide your real name, write in a fake address, fake your birth date, and never give your true income. If you're single, write that you're married, and vice versa. If asked for the number of your children, never give the correct number. If asked for hobbies and interests, always remember that this isn't from casual curiosity, and falsify the information.

Some of these soft-core scammers appeal to you by stating that with accurate and detailed information about your lifestyle, you'll be "protected" from receiving ads that aren't applicable to you. Some will even promise that, with a tightly focused profile of your lifestyle and interests, you'll receive fewer ads. Don't believe this for a minute. Fake your information and scam them the way they're trying to scam you.

In answering these questionnaires, always understate your income as a basic step. Merchandisers are interested in people who have lots of money to spend, not those living marginally. They know that if you have a lot of discretionary income, you're more likely to buy a VCR or sound system than if you're living hand to mouth.

Viruses

The Melissa Virus and other recent ones have gotten a lot of publicity because they have been so widespread and have disabled so many computers. Unfortunately, only partial protection is available against these viruses. The reason is that creating viruses is a form of electronic warfare, and there's always a back-and-forth dynamic operating. What this means, in simple language, is that as soon as someone develops a countermeasure against a new virus, someone else creates a virus to defeat that countermeasure.

There are anti-virus programs available from several sources. You can take your pick of several offered in computer and office supply stores. The problem is that these anti-virus programs protect only against viruses already known, and new ones appear regularly. You have to keep updating them. Still, when a new virus appears, your anti-virus program may not defeat it.

A basic security measure is not to open any attachment to any e-mail from someone you don't know. Opening the attachment is often the triggering mechanism needed to activate the virus.

Another is to use an e-mail program less likely to be attacked. Many viruses are aimed at users of Microsoft Outlook, and using Netscape will make you less vulnerable.

Cards and Card Numbers

You should exercise caution in regard to the Personal Identification Number (PIN) for your Automatic Teller Machine (ATM) card. This is often a four- or five-digit number. Do not write it on your ATM card, because this is the kiss of death if anyone finds your wallet. If you worry about forgetting it, you can carry it in your wallet, but disguised. Write it down as part of a telephone number. Make it harder for a thief by writing it backwards. For example, if your PIN number is "3066" write it as "292-6603." This works best if you keep a list of telephone numbers in your wallet, as you can insert your PIN as the number of a fictitious person, such as "John Smith: 292-6603."

Another basic security technique that few observe is to notify credit card companies and banks well in advance of any address changes. The reason? You don't want your credit card and other statements lying around in your old mailbox where almost anyone might find them. The sensitive information they contain, especially your account numbers, are too precious to risk.

You should also be aware of the billing cycle of any credit card account you have. The reason is that fraud artists who steal your financial identity will also file change of addresses with the credit card companies. This is to prevent the victim from becoming aware that fraudulent charges are appearing on his statement, giving the scam artists a few days or weeks grace period before the victim finds out and has the cards deactivated. If your credit card, banking statement, or other financial documents are more than a few days overdue, call the company and investigate. Ask if there's been an address change filed recently, and if so, ask to speak with someone in the security department.

Many banks and credit card providers are aware of this stratagem, and have developed a simple countermeasure to foil it. Many, when they receive a change of address, will mail an acknowledgement to both the new and old addresses. That way, the customer is aware of the change of address and can notify the bank or credit card provider if it's spurious.

One way of ensuring mail security and security for other materials and purchases you receive is to use a private mail drop. This is a commercial mail receiving service operating under a name such as "Mail N More," "Mail Boxes, Etc." or something similar. Mail drops will receive mail for you, allowing you to pick it up at your convenience. They also receive packages from UPS and FEDEX, as well as Parcel Post, so if you order goods to be delivered to you, you don't have to worry about their being left outside your front door, open to theft. They offer much more security than a locked mailbox because there's always someone there. This is especially important when you order checks, as a thief can steal them and write many spurious checks in your name before you become aware that your new checks are overdue.

Another security tactic is to contact the bank or credit card provider at once if you lose your card or cards. Next, contact the police, to get it on record. As we've seen, the local police are not much help at fighting credit card and Internet fraud, but they are useful when you need to get a piece of official paper into the system, to substantiate your loss.

Another precaution is never to leave credit cards or other sensitive documents in your car. Your car can be stolen, or fall victim to "auto burglars," thieves who don't steal the vehicle but rummage through it in search of valuables.[2]

With all that, one way of reducing your risk is simply to reduce the number of bank and credit card accounts you maintain. We've seen credit card wallets with huge arrays of plastic pockets that hold a dozen or more credit cards. Each is a liability for several reasons. Each is vulnerable to theft. Each account provider must be notified if the wallet is lost or stolen.

Learn to pay cash for many purchases. Each credit card purchase results in a charge slip, which you must safeguard or destroy to prevent its falling into the hands of a fraud artist. Carry $100 or more in your wallet for grocery purchases, etc. That way, if you lose your wallet, you're only out the amount of cash in it, not many thousands of dollars' potential loss from credit card misuse.

Okay, so maybe you can't get rid of all your credit cards because of the convenience they provide. At a gas station, for example, it's a lot easier to insert your credit card into the pump to pay, instead of going inside and standing in line with other customers. If you pay for gas by credit card, always take your receipt. Keep in mind that, while some pumps will prompt you by asking if you want a receipt, many do this automatically. Also, some will print a receipt whether you say "yes" or "no" because of a software defect. Always check the receipt slot, because one may be popping out, and you don't want to leave it for someone else to pick up.

Online Merchants

If you order merchandise over the Internet, be careful of scam artists. There are many legitimate companies selling online today, and some of these are well known. Amazon.com, for example, sells books, tapes, and CD-ROMs over the Internet, as does Barnes & Noble. However, be extra careful when responding to an ad on the Internet, especially if it's spam. If you receive an ad from a vendor, check him out before replying. There are several Internet telephone directories, and you can use these to verify that the company actually exists and has a physical address. You may also want to check him out with the National Fraud Information Center by calling (800) 876-7060.

Be especially careful if the vendor is pressuring you for a quick order. If he exhorts you to make up your mind right now, take that as a warning. Another danger sign is an anonymous e-mail address (see below) because this may denote a fly-by-night operator.

If you operate a business online, be watchful for Internet fraud. Learn some basic facts about fraud artists, such as their practice of operating across state lines, and of ordering merchandise on "rush" orders. Putting a rush on the order gets the merchandise into their hands faster, because they are in a race with time. They have to get the goods and get away before the victim realizes that his card's missing and has it canceled. Watch for orders where the shipping charges seem high for the merchandise. Keep in mind that fraud artists want the goods delivered quickly, and really don't worry about shipping charges because they're not the ones who will have to pay them.

Be careful when accepting orders that come from free e-mail services, such as JUNO. Scammers can easily set up an e-mail address under an alias, making it almost totally untraceable. There are many free e-mail services, and not all are immediately obvious. One way to check is to type "www." in front of the domain name of your customer's e-mail address into your browser. For example, if you receive an order from jjones@flash.net you type www.flash.net into your browser, and you'll quickly discover that Flashnet is a legitimate online service. To get a Flashnet e-mail address, the customer has to have an account. If, however, you find that you end up at a site that has free e-mail accounts, you have reason to further verify the order.

There are some tell-tale signs of scams. One is when the "ship to" address is different from the billing address. One defense is to require anyone who orders the goods shipped to a different address to send you a fax with his signature and credit card number. This pins him down to a specific phone number, which provides a better "handle" on him than an e-mail address. Many online merchants leave themselves wide open to fraud because they don't even ask for a billing address if the customer furnishes a credit card number.

Watch for unusual orders, such as those larger than average, and those specifying quick delivery, such as overnight air. If the shipping cost is larger than the value of the order, be extra careful. Also be careful with orders shipped out of the country. Remember that an order can originate from literally anywhere in the world, and that a scammer who places a fraudulent order from another country and orders delivery there is totally out of the reach of law enforcement.

Ask for the customer's telephone number on all orders. This will allow you to call to verify the order if you're suspicious. If it's a new number, you may be dealing with a criminal boiler room.

If worst comes to worst, and you discover that you've been scammed by an online customer, one defense is to notify the service provider's security department, which can shut down the fraud artist's account quickly.

There are several emerging methods to reduce online and other types of high-tech fraud. One is the digital signature, which is an encrypted segment of software that ensures that the person sending the message or order really is the person he or she claims to be.

Another security method is biometrics, which includes fingerprinting and eye retina scanning, for positive identification. This is limited to situations where the client is making the transaction in person, such as withdrawing money from a bank account at the counter. Given the state of the art, biometrics does not adapt well to online transactions.

Authentication is the use of an electronic code to identify the person or company making the transaction. This can be the customer's mother's maiden name, for example, or other information the fraud artist is unlikely to know.

Using common-sense tactics can make it much harder for scam artists to victimize you. Always remember that some of the sharpest minds in the world are constantly working, figuring the angles, to separate you from your money by using insidious methods.

Never forget that many modern fraud artists have figured the angles, and have devised methods that are not illegal according to today's laws. This means that you have little or no recourse if you're victimized, and that reporting them to law enforcement agencies will do no good. This is why you always have to be on your guard, because you're truly the first line of defense against fraud.

Notes:

1. Personal acquaintance of the author.
2. Pettinari, Cmdr. Dave, "The Basics of Investigating Credit Card Fraud on the Internet," *Police & Security News*, May/June 2000, p. 63.

Appendix One
Resources

There are resources available to help you avoid fraud, and to help you recover if you've fallen victim to fraud. A point to emphasize is that prevention is far better than reaction where fraud is involved.

Your local police department is the first step. The agency may have an "anti-crime" officer who provides useful advice to citizens seeking to insulate themselves against fraud artists and other criminals. However, if you've become victim to a sophisticated fraud effort that crosses state lines, you're likely to get no help from local police. Some agencies are so disorganized that all you'll get is a run-around. You'll find yourself shunted from one clerk to another, with each claiming that the responsibility lies with another division. This is especially true if you've been the victim of an Internet fraud and the agency has no officer familiar with computer crimes.

Your state attorney general's office is a slightly better prospect for help. The state attorney general typically has a consumer fraud division, which specializes in this type of crime. They can usually provide honest answers. How much practical help you'll receive in recovering whatever you've lost is another matter.

Overall, there is no absolute protection against fraud artists. You may or may not be able to recover what a con artist has scammed from you, and you may or may not succeed in finding the scammer and having him prosecuted. You are your own first line of defense, and the best defense is prevention.

Other Organizations

The Better Business Bureau web site is:
www.bbb.org/bureaus

This can provide the address of your local office, and other information. The Yellow Pages provide a quicker source for the BBB's local address and phone number, though.

Note that the BBB is a private, volunteer organization with absolutely no police powers. Also, fraud artists are hardly likely to register with the BBB. The main function of the BBB is prevention by informing people of current con games they may encounter.

Another BBB web site is:

www.bbbonline.org

This site provides tips on online shopping, as well as other valuable consumer information.

A blacklist of Internet advertisers is found at:

http://math-www.uni-paderborn.de/~axel/bl/blacklist.html

Consumer World:
www.consumerworld.org

Federal Trade Commission:

www.ftc.gov/bcp/conline/edcams/supplies

This FTC web site deals with office supply scams, and is worth a close look if you're a small businessman vulnerable to this type of fraud.

Fraudnet, the Association of Certified Fraud Examiners:

www.acfe.org/

Internet Scambusters:

www.scambusters.com

This site is a gold mine of information because it has many pages dealing with different kinds of scams, but an array of links to other sites that deal directly or tangentially with frauds, scams, and hoaxes. Some are U.S. Government web sites, while others are private organizations. There is information on real and hoax viruses, urban legends, spam, and other time-wasters and threats.

Department of Energy Computer Incident Advisory Capability:

http://ciac.llnl.gov/ciac/CIACHoaxes.html

This is a D.O.E. web site that provides the latest information on computer virus hoaxes. It's worth checking out a message you receive from a friend before forwarding it to other friends, because he may have innocently forwarded a hoax to you.

A related site dealing with chain letters is:

http://ciac.llnl.gov/ciac/CIACChainLetters.html

Many well-meaning people will forward a chain letter because they've received it from a friend.

For urban legends, check out this site:

www.urbanlegends.com

This site lists various urban legends, and you can discover whether the horrifying story you've just read is a phony one that has already made the rounds.

Another urban legend site is:

> http://urbanlegends.about.com

This performs a similar function.

National Fraud Investigations Center:

> www.tunfc.com

U.S. Postal Service:

> www.Usps.gov/websites/depart/insept/consmenu.htm

FBI Computer Crime Center:

> www.fbi.gov/compcrim.htm

Scams on the Internet:

> www.ftc.gov/bcp/scams01.htm

Appendix Two
Glossary

Back Door: A simple password left in the computer to enable a service technician to gain easy access. The danger is that the same password will provide access to many computers, very much the way a passkey permits opening many locks in a series.

Blocked Call: An anonymous phone call that does not show the name and number of the caller on your Caller ID. This can be because the caller has an unlisted number, or because he's using electronic trickery to avoid having his number posted.

Boiler Room: An office with many telephones used by telemarketers and fraud artists. A boiler room used for legitimate telemarketing has a regular staff, a fixed address, and remains in place for a long time. Boiler rooms employed for fraud are on very short-term leases, use rented furniture, and change locations frequently. It's impossible to tell which type of boiler room a telemarketer is using by the phone call. You have to infer this from the contents of the call. If it sounds too good to be true, it probably is.

Grooming: Techniques used systematically by child molesters for meeting and gaining the confidence of children online. This shows the importance of knowing where your children browse on the Internet.

Handle: A pseudonym used by someone in an Internet chat room or posting to a bulletin board to preserve anonymity. While many who use handles do so merely to protect their privacy, especially when chatting on sexual topics, some handles are used by scammers. Never take anyone you meet on the Internet at face value.

Identity Theft: Impersonating someone to conduct fraudulent transactions. This can be by stealing his credit card number and expiration date, bank account numbers, passwords, and other sensitive information.

Investor Push: The rise in price of a stock because investors are actively trading in it. This can result from a stock's strength, or it can be stimulated by scam artists seeking to hype a stock as part of a pump and dump scheme.

Mailbox Raider: A thief who specializes in stealing mail out of mailboxes. They tend to prey on curbside mailboxes that are unlocked and therefore allow quick and easy access. This practice isn't new, as for decades mailbox raiders stole Social Security and welfare checks from mailboxes. They knew that checks typically arrived during the first three days of the month, and concentrated their efforts then. Today, they're also after checks written to pay utility bills, and they steal from mailboxes throughout the month. They also go after credit card statements, from which they can glean the victim's account number.

    This has resulted in the post office's installing locking mailboxes in new developments. The locks will not stop a totally determined thief, but will slow down the casual mailbox raider enough so that he'll seek out unlocked mailboxes.

Mail Drop: A private mail receiving service. A mail drop offers much more security than a curbside mailbox or even a locked mailbox.

Oversubscribing: Accepting more customers than the facility can handle, often for a "lifetime membership," by offering an attractive and unrealistic price. This is good for cash flow in the short run, at the expense of customers who get shortchanged on service.

Password: An alphanumeric sequence (it can be an actual word) that allows access to a computer or a secure area within it. The computer prompts for the password, and if the user enters the correct one, will allow access. A sophisticated computer security program will allow three tries. After three incorrect tries, the computer will lock up, shut down, or notify the company security department. This is to prevent "brute force" efforts at entering the password by trying different combinations.

Push Poll: A spurious telephone poll used to discredit an opponent, used by some unscrupulous candidates.

Spam: Electronic junk mail. You are vulnerable to spam only if you have e-mail. E-mail services differ in their policies against spam. Some are very effective, while others leave you wide open to spamming. Your Internet browsing practices also affect the volume of spam you receive. If you participate in chat rooms and other discussion groups, you'll be leaving your electronic signature for spammers to collect, and you can expect more spam than if you were more discreet.

Trojan Horse: A program you inadvertently download that does things without your knowledge. Some Trojan horses send copies of your files back over the Internet to a snooper, among other things. The most destructive and malicious Trojan horses spread viruses, taking over your e-mail to send copies to all in your address book.

Unbundling: Charging separately for minor items connected with a product or service. A flagrant example of this is the hospital that charges patients five dollars for an aspirin.

Virus: A series of computer codes that instruct the receiving computer to do odd things, such as display a joke message on the screen, send a copy of the virus attached to each outgoing e-mail, etc. Some viruses are merely pranks, while others are outright vicious, erasing the host computer's hard drive or performing other destructive acts.

Appendix Three
Abbreviations Used in Personal Ads

Most personal ads contain abbreviations to save space and the cost of words. Mainstream abbreviations are the following:

S	Single
D	Divorced
WF	White Female
WM	White Male
HM	Hispanic Male
BM	Black Male
NA	Native American
NBM	Never Been Married
ISO	In Search Of
LTR	Long Term Relationship
BBW	Big Beautiful Woman
SP	Single Parent
P	Professional
C	Christian
J	Jewish
NS	Non Smoker
LD	Light Drinker
ND	Non Drinker or No Drugs
NDU	Non Drug User

It's pretty clear that these abbreviations can be ambiguous, even without a conscious intent to deceive. Defining "Long Term Relationship" will bring different answers from different people. What, exactly, does "Professional" mean? "C" stands for "Christian," but there are hundreds of denominations. "SP" means "Single Parent," but doesn't specify how many children or their ages. "BBW," Big Beautiful Woman, usually means someone who weighs more than average. This is why it's important to understand that ads are only a beginning. Follow-up is important, to clarify the picture.

Placing ads for exotic tastes follows the same basic pattern as mainstream ads. However, getting into exotic sex brings a different set of practices. Are you looking for a correspondent, erotic telephone talk, or something else? You'll have to choose your terms to match. This brings another group of abbreviations:

A	Active
P	Passive
A/P	Active/Passive
BB	Body Builder
B&D	Bondage and Discipline or Bondage and Domination
Bi	Bisexual
BJ	Blow Job
C&B	Cock & Balls
CBT	Cock & Ball Torture
CC	Clean Cut (can mean either well-groomed or circumcised)
FF	Fist Fucking
Fr	French (oral sex)
Gr	Greek (anal sex)
G	Gay, as in GWM (Gay White Male)
GS	Golden Shower (urine streams)
JO	"Jerk Off," masturbation
J/O	(same as above)
LM	Latin Male

MWM	Married White Male
P/A	Prince Albert (a ring through the bottom of the glans penis)
SM	Sado-masochism
S/M	(same as above)
TS	Transsexual
TT	Tit Torture
TV	Transvestite (cross-dresser)
U/C	Uncut, Uncircumcised
VA	Verbal Abuse
WS	Water Sports (Urine)

As with mainstream ads, several abbreviations have ambiguous or multiple meanings, and it's important to interpret them in the light of the context. Try to make your terms as clear as possible, for example; "Phone J/O," "Exchange underwear," etc.

YOU WILL ALSO WANT TO READ:

☐ **19169 TAKE NO PRISONERS, Destroying Enemies with Dirty and Malicious Tricks,** *by Mack Nasty.* Mack Nasty doesn't believe in holding a grudge. He believes in swift, sure and devastating retribution. In this book, Mack reveals the most deliciously despicable revenge techniques ever conceived, including how to destroy your enemy's house or car and how to get someone arrested for drug trafficking, kiddie porn, firearms violations or product tampering. *Sold for entertainment purposes only. 1990, 5½ x 8½, 118 pp, soft cover.* **$12.95.**

☐ **61163 IDENTITY THEFT, The Cybercrime of the Millennium,** *by John. Q. Newman.* Your most valuable possession is what makes you *you* — your identity. What would happen if someone stole it? Each year, more than 500,000 Americans fall victim to identity theft, and that number is rising. In this comprehensive book, you will learn: how thieves use computer networks and other information sources to adopt, use, and subsequently ravage the identities of unsuspecting victims; what you can do to protect yourself from identity theft, and how to fight back effectively if you are one of the unlucky victims. *1999, 5½ x 8½, 106 pp, soft cover.* **$12.00.**

☐ **61168 THE ID FORGER: Birth Certificates & Other Documents Explained,** *by John Q. Newman. The ID Forger* covers in step-by-step detail all of the classic and modern high-tech methods of forging the commonly used identification documents. Chapters include: The use of homemade documents; Old-fashioned forgery; Computer forgery; Birth certificate basics; and Other miscellaneous document forgery. *1999, 5½ x 8½, 110 pp, soft cover.* **$15.00.**

☐ **19146 YOUR REVENGE IS IN THE MAIL,** *by Keith Wade.* There are a lot of jerks in the world that need to be taught a lesson. The problem is, how to get to them without causing yourself a lot of trouble? The answer is in this book. More than 60 letters you can copy and use to get even. *Sold for side-splitting entertainment purposes only. 1988, 5½ x 8½, 168 pp, soft cover.* **$12.95.**

☐ **61152 DOCUMENT FRAUD AND OTHER CRIMES OF DECEPTION,** *by Jesse M. Greenwald.* Written by a 20-year practitioner of document fraud with 22 felonies and five prison terms to his credit, this book clearly explains: computer equipment the forger needs and alternative methods of acquiring it; necessary software; how the forgers fabricate checks, stock certificates, trust and quit-claim deeds, vehicle titles, and bonded credit cards; methods the forger employs to obtain alternative identification; and much, much more. *1997, 5½ x 8½, 152 pp, illustrated, soft cover.* **$15.00.**

☐ **10066 HOW TO USE MAIL DROPS FOR PROFIT, PRIVACY AND SELF-PROTECTION, Second Edition,** *by Jack Luger.* There are many reasons you might want to use a mail drop; nomads use no fixed address; if your mail has been stolen from your residential mailbox; to keep creditors and correspondents at arm's length; to keep you actual whereabouts secret, and much more. Mail drops are the number one most important technique for insuring your privacy. They are confidential mailing addresses that allow you to receive and send mail anonymously. This book contains several lists by state and city. It belongs in the library of anyone concerned about his privacy. *1996, 5½ x 8½, 184 pp, soft cover.* **$16.95.**

☐ **58080 THE PRIVACY POACHERS, How the Government and Big Corporations Gather, Use and Sell Information About You,** *by Tony Lesce.* This book explains how various snoops get their hands on sensitive information about you, such as your financial records, medical history, legal records, and much more. Government and private snoops can combine data from financial transactions by using taps, mail monitoring, and other surveillance methods. This information is then packaged and sold, over and over and over again, without your consent. Find out what the Privacy Poachers have on you, and what you can do to protect yourself. *1992, 5½ x 8½, 155 pp, soft cover.* **$16.95.**

- **19106 POISON PEN LETTERS, *by Keith Wade*.** A complete guide to getting revenge through the mail. If you've had problems with people or organizations that seem too big to fight back against, this book is for you. Covers retaliation against individuals, corporations and even government agencies. Includes nearly 100 letters, along with tips on stationery, mailing, and how to keep from getting caught. *Sold for informational purposes only. 1984, 5½ x 8½, 103 pp, soft cover.* **$12.95.**

- **10052 CODE MAKING AND CODE BREAKING, *by Jack Luger*.** We live in an information age; information is bought, sold, and stolen like other goods. Businesses and individuals are learning to keep their secrets safe with this practical, illustrated guide to building and busting codes. Learn how to construct simple and complex codes. Learn how computers are used to make and break codes. Learn why the most unbreakable code isn't always the best. Ideal for those interested in professional and personal privacy. This book is a must-read for those who want to keep their secrets safe. *1990, 5½ x 8½, 125 pp, illustrated, soft cover.* **$12.95.**

- **61129 UNDERSTANDING U.S. IDENTITY DOCUMENTS, *by* John Q. Newman.** The most detailed examination of identity documents ever published. This guide is a must for all new-identity seekers and anyone interested in identification, false identification and alternate ID. You know who you are, but thousands of people you deal with in government and business know you only from a document. If you alter your documents, you can evade taxes, regulation and supervision. This book covers birth certificates, Social Security cards, driver's licenses, and passports. It shows how each document is generated and used; it explains the strengths and weaknesses of the agencies issuing them. *1991, 8½ x 11, 207 pp, illustrated, soft cover.* **$27.95.**

*We offer the very finest in controversial and unusual books? — A complete catalog is sent **FREE** with every book order. If you would like to order the catalog separately, please see our ad on the last page of this book.*

Please send me the books I have marked below:

- ☐ 19212, 21st Century Revenge, $15.00
- ☐ 19209, Out of Business, $17.95
- ☐ 19193, Gaslighting, $14.95
- ☐ 19169, Take No Prisoners, $12.95
- ☐ 61163, Identity Theft, $12.00
- ☐ 61168, The ID Forger, $15.00
- ☐ 19146, Your Revenge is in the Mail, $12.95
- ☐ 61152, Document Fraud, $15.00
- ☐ 10066, How to Use Mail Drops, $16.95
- ☐ 58080, The Privacy Poachers, $16.95
- ☐ 19106, Poison Pen Letters, $12.95
- ☐ 10052, Code Making and Code Breaking, $12.95
- ☐ 61129, Understanding U.S. Identity Documents, $27.95.
- ☐ 88888, The Best Book Catalog in the World, $5.00

21FR2

LOOMPANICS UNLIMITED
PO BOX 1197
PORT TOWNSEND, WA 98368

I am enclosing $ _____ which includes $4.95 for shipping and handling of orders up to $25.00. Add $1.00 for each additional $25.00 ordered. *Washington residents please include 7.9% for sales tax.*

NAME_____

ADDRESS _____

CITY_____

STATE/ZIP_____

We accept Visa, Discover, and MasterCard.
To place a credit card order *only,* call 1-800-380-2230
24 hours a day, 7 days a week.

Check out our Web site: www.loompanics.com